LOVE

Mary Jan and Lawrence J. Losoncy

Ave Maria Press
Notre Dame, Indiana 46556

Library of Congress Catalog Card Number: 75-130460
ISBN 0-87793-025-2
© 1970 by Ave Maria Press. All rights reserved
Printed in the United States of America
Photography: Cover and pages 142/143 **Bruce Roberts**
pages 6/7 **David Schlaver, CSC**
8, 30 **Jay Steinberg,** 14 **Bro Martinus, CSC**
13, 21, 29, 38, 47, 66, 74, 93, 102, 111,
118, 126, 133 **Justin Soleta**
22, 39, 48/49, 58/59, 94 **Rohn Engh**
67, 141 **Vern Sigl,** 75 **Terry Barrett**
84, 112, 119, 127 **Philip Curry**
103 **Bryan Moss,** 134 **Rose Farkas**

Contents

Foreword

This is a book for young people about love. Not the abstract notions of love, not poetry, but just some thoughts about everyday love, the kind of love that goes into a date, into a marriage, into a family: the kind of love that makes people important to one another.

The pages which follow are intended as a sharing of our reflections on love after a few years of marriage. So many things have been written of love and about love, so much has been painted, so many movies have been made, and so many poems have been created under the inspiration of love, that a book such as this cannot pretend to have anything new. But what it does have is the testimony of personal experience.

Almost every chapter reflects our philosophy of love, a philosophy which of necessity must be highly personal. We speak of the meaning and beauty of love as we see it from the early dating stage in life to the early parenthood stage of life. We in no way are trying to teach about love because love is something which can only be learned and lived; we certainly are not bragging about our love, which has had its ups and downs after four years of marriage and two children. We are merely reflecting upon what we have experienced and what we see others experiencing. One of the most characteristic marks of lovers is that they wish to share their happiness with others, and that is all we are trying to do in these pages.

Mary Jan and Lawrence J. Losoncy

1.

A TIME FOR LOVING AND A TIME FOR LIVING . . .

If you are 20 years old this year, you were born nine years after the American Pacific fleet sank at Pearl Harbor.

One million Chinese were pouring over the Yalu River that year, sweeping across Korea.

America was entering its third year of the Korean war.

When you were one year old General Eisenhower became President.

When you were four years old colored TV was just catching on.

When you started first grade, nuclear submarines were just being designed.

When you were in the third grade, America started a space program and the St. Lawrence Seaway was completed.

When you were in junior high school Pope John was dying.

When you were starting high school a man had flown a spaceship for a few hours.

Since you were born, one billion other people were born.

Since you were born, the United States has had five Presidents.

The Catholic Church has had three popes.

Thirty-four new nations have been born in Africa.

During the time you were in high school, over two million Ibos died of starvation in Biafra.

If you are 19, your grandmother and grandfather lived before radio was invented and your grandchildren will take trips back and forth from Venus.

Our world is changing.

Change never just "happens." People change our world, and will continue to change our world, whether we like it or not. The only real question is whether we want the world to be the way other people make it or to be the way *we* make it. Our choice is to shape the world we live in or to go along with whatever happens and make the best of it. But nobody can do anything until they know what it is they want. How can we make our world the way we want it to be until we know what we want it to be?

It isn't just you and I who ask ourselves what we want from life. Every human asks and answers this question whenever important decisions come up . . . and important decisions keep coming up. Graduation, marriage, new jobs, a man and woman's first child, sickness, death, friendship, every event drives us to ask again and again what it is we want from life.

Life is such a precarious affair. Whether

10

we ask ourselves what we want from it or not, life is short and ends suddenly, surprisingly, remorsefully. We have all known people who, in spite of the shortness and uncertainty of life, managed to make a place in life, managed to achieve something great. The Kennedy brothers were two such people. So was Martin Luther King. So was Malcolm X. So were any number of people going all the way back to the dark corners of history.

But no matter how great or how much even the greatest people have managed to be and to accomplish, they have all nevertheless died. While they were alive, their accomplishments were not the things which made them great. What made them great was something inside of them, something which for want of a better description, is known as love.

Accomplishments do not build a personality, and the things we do are not the reason for our relationships to people. Our Lord once said, in so many words, that it really would not do much good to gain the whole world if we lost our soul. Translated, that could also mean that all the accomplishments in the world are not enough to make us happy.

Happiness is an accident. It is not something that can be gained or bought or made or kept. It is an aftereffect, something that happens when we aren't looking, when we don't notice. It is a spillover from love. The only way to be happy is to love, and when we love we really are not thinking of ourselves or of happiness at all. Though happiness is an accident, however, love is not. Nor is love an afterthought. It is deliberate and controllable. But when we love, happiness follows every time. That is why love is the music of life and the source of beautiful, enduring, distinctive melodies.

Not all the melodies of life are happy ones, and not everyone feels like singing when it's all over. Not everyone has unlimited success. But every person can be a success by his own standards, if he has standards.

In a growing, changing, challenging world, we all have a wide choice of careers, of marriage partners, of belief, and of values. But no matter how wide a choice and how many options, we must choose. Each person's melody of life must be his own and will be his own. There is no stealing tunes because each person is able to sing only his own tune.

One man in our lifetime wrote and lived his melody of life so clearly it will never die. His name was Robert Kennedy and his notion of love is summed up in something he once said, something we have seen in the writing of this book as a reflection of the Gospel and as an ideal which will always shame but inspire us:

> . . . *Each time a man stands for an ideal*
> *or acts to improve the lot of others*
> *or strikes out against injustice*
> *he sends forth a ripple*
> *of hope . . .*

For Openers....

Can you think of four significant events which changed the world during the first four years of your life?

Who do you think are the ten most influential people in the world today and why are they influential?

If you had absolute or even divine power, what is the one thing you would most want to change in the world today?

If you could be God for one minute, what would you do? If you could be the President of the United States for one thousand days as was John Kennedy, what would you do?

TURN AROUND

Turn around and look at me! Isn't that one of the things we really want people to do? We live in a country where everyone turns around to stare at the girl with a big chest, the student with a brilliant mind, movie stars, the famous, handsome, successful, rich people. No one notices old people, poor people, stupid people, unattractive people, little people, and people like us. The unlucky ones are most of us, and our unluckiness is that we are just ordinary.

The trouble with us "ordinary" people is that we act ordinary for so long that we start thinking we are ordinary. We find out how wrong we are when we fall in love. The little child who struts around showing off has more sense than we do! Even the rooster wouldn't be able to let out a decent crow if it weren't for a sense of importance. Jesus once said about this matter that God loves the sparrows so much that he notices when one of them falls to earth. Then he added, "and you, how much more than sparrows is your worth!"

Sometimes we don't use any more sense than sparrows. We cut people down, we treat them like toys for our own pleasure or like machines which have no feelings. Sometimes the way we cut ourselves down is even worse. If we don't believe we are important, who else will?

Everybody else knows we are worth something. They know we are a human being for whom two parents sacrificed a great deal. They know we are a person for whom God died. They know we are intelligent, alive, personable, and an individual worthy of love and esteem. But do *we* realize this? It is when this realization begins to dawn upon us that we open up to others and seek their love. This is what makes people notice us. When we open up to them we let them see how we think and what we are interested in. We, in turn, begin to see their worth and to assert their value. Our attractiveness in other people's estimation no longer depends on our figure or on our looks, but on what we really are. When we start turning around to see ourselves and to look at others, we're going to be amazed by all the people staring at us.

Love Is the Big Thing

To fall in love with someone else is to take ourselves seriously. We are saying we have found someone of extraordinary value and we are offering ourself to them. If the love is for real, the offer is forever. There's just no bigger compliment to pay than to fall in love with someone. It's the ultimate in human relationships. It's the ultimate in happiness. It's the highest value we can place on ourself and on someone else.

Everyone lives for love. Is there anything else more worthwhile than to love somebody? Can you think of anything you want more than to be loved, especially by one person who will love you completely, emotionally, physically, totally, and uniquely? We literally live for love. It's got to be the greatest thrill around, and without love, life would be impossible. A lot of people can make a good case for saying that not only is love the greatest thing going, it's the only thing going. That particular outlook is a fair summary of the point of view Christ presented. It is also characteristic of many philosophers, particularly some of the existentialists. It represents the thinking of many Eastern philosophers. It's something to think about. Love does not come easily. No one will love us until they notice us. For a boy that means no girl is going to go for you until she sees you, and she's not going to see you just because you're there. For a girl, that means no guy is going to get serious until he knows who you are, and he won't know who you are until you let him know. We all need to be noticed and we all want to be noticed because we are hungry for love in one form or another. If love is the biggest thing in life, being noticed has to be the second biggest thing. But how can we be noticed if we are convinced that we are nobody? What's the use if only the richest, sexiest, smartest, and coolest are worthy of attention? Even they will not be rich, sexy, brilliant and cool forever, and what then? Who will be loved in later life if personality and the real man or woman underneath the appearance don't really matter?

For Love You Need People

People who need people are the luckiest people of all. They're lucky because their need is leading them right to the one source of happiness built into being human.

"I love the human race, it's just people I can't stand." Anyone who figures he can live by loving the human race is stupid. If we can't love people, we can't love. Usually we agree that people who need people are lucky, and that most of us, being unlucky, can't stand people. Or at least, can't stand many people. What we never realize is that *everyone* needs people all the time.

The big pitch to us is that we need God, teachers, doctors, priests, laws, rules, money, jobs, and so on. But common sense tells us we need *people!* People who care! Look at a child and see how much he or she wants to be loved. With love, even a sick child can be happy. Without love, given freely all the time, a child is not happy. It's that simple, and the need for love is a need which grows and grows.

Love begins in our life as a one-way thing. We take all the love we can get, and it comes in the form of food, warmth, comfort. As babies, we demand to be held, to be cuddled, and to be fed. As toddlers we also demand to be played with, to be talked to, to be noticed. All this time our parents, our brothers and sisters, and our friends give us love. We just drink it all in. Children die when they are not loved. But so do adults. In fact, adults without love die faster.

Our craving for love of every sort grows by leaps and bounds. That's why we hate being alone; that's why when our parents don't care about us we go wild with panic. That's why it's up-setting to leave home. That's why it is so tragic when our parents die.

The people-need is in fact two-sided. We need the love of people in order to live and to grow. But we also need to love other people if they are to live and to grow. The really odd thing is that when we just take everyone else's love, we grow to be a freak, a human sponge that can only suck up everyone around.

The Unreal Split:
Loving and Being Loved

Most of us have been pretty well bombarded with the notion that love means to love other people, and that our duty lies in that direction. From the time a child is able to walk until he is full-grown in our culture, he is constantly told that to be a respectable Christian and a decent human being he must love other people, he must help other people, he must do this and do that.
At the same time, he is also bombarded with another notion of love. We have all experienced this other bombardment, the one that says sex is everything, the one that urges us to take everything we can get, eat everything we can see, earn every dollar available, get the most out of life and get it fast. This is the bombardment that tells the child, from the time he can under-stand, that he should take all he can get and that he won't get anything he doesn't take. Two different messages about love, and both true! But because they are split, we are asked to make

19

a choice. To make a choice for either half of love is fatal.

Love does not come in parts. We have heard that love means to get everything we can out of life, especially sexually. We have also heard that love means to help and to serve other people. In order to love at all, we must both give and get, sexually and all other ways. Love is a two-way process or there is no love at all. There is no choice between loving and being loved. No choice between taking from people or giving to people. It's all part of the same thing. We need people for what they do to us and for what we do for them. We need to love and we need to be loved. To make a choice between one or the other is to accept a split that makes love impossible.

To say we need people is to say a mouthful. People who need people are indeed lucky. And we all need people. We need them both ways.

What do you say...

Can you describe the way you remember someone you know well when they were in love — — — an older brother, a sister or a friend?

How much do you think you are worth?

Who are the five people you need most in life?

Can you name three people who need you more than anyone else in their lives?

3.

BEING ATTRACTIVE

If you are a man, women are the most interesting thing about life. From boyhood until burial, the male psychology is one of fascination, obsession, and possession. Put a man in a wildlife preserve and he'll notice the female guide. Let a man be standing along a parade route and he'll notice the girls before anything else. Go on a date with a man and he'll notice you constantly, sizing you up and thinking about you.

This is not to say that men are sexual beasts or that the male psychology leads men to excess. It is simply to observe that in the male thinking, women are at least one half of life. It is natural and normal for this to happen during high school and college, for it is during these years that sexual feelings are the strongest.

In the earlier years of life, a boy will likely

be more immature in his thinking about the opposite sex than will a girl of the same age. This is also true in high school, since girls mature a little faster than boys until the end of high school. A man in high school is still trying to figure out the facts of life. He is still trying to figure out why one girl's personality turns him on so much, when another girl's personality doesn't do anything for him. He is still puzzled, many times, about how to relate to women and what to say around them. He can no longer take women for granted.

When you ask a man to talk about women, you won't get much. It's harder for men to say what they think on a topic like this. When you ask a man in high school what he thinks, you may not get anything at all.

What Does a Man Look For?

We asked a number of boys in high school what they thought about girls. They really didn't want to discuss it very much. We asked them what they looked for in their girlfriends and what traits they thought a man looked for in a woman generally. They finally agreed to write down what they thought, rather than to talk about it.

Many of their comments concerned the physical appearance, the measurements, and the sexual attraction they expected of their girl-friends. Even though they wrote on the spur of the moment, what they wrote was sad, really. They showed a concentration on women as sexual playthings, a concentration which is fairly typical in many high schools and colleges in our country today. It's hardly a compliment to a woman to view her totally in terms of sex.

It's sad and it's hardly human.

But there were other comments which showed a concern for character and personality and relationships. What do boys look for in girls besides sex? Here are some of the comments:

"A girl that has feeling. Someone to make you feel worthwhile."

"A cute face. A good personality."

"Fine personality. Intelligence."

"I want her to like what I like."

"I think a woman is a woman when she doesn't like to tower over a man. When she shows all her love to the man she loves. When she doesn't complain. When she makes herself beautiful for the man she loves and does whatever she can to please him."

"Besides courtesy, politeness and neatness in appearance, her creativity, humor, considerateness and sensitivity are what really count."

"A girl should be feminine: She should be gentle and sensitive and affectionate. She should be able to make people happy just to be around her."

"She shouldn't be hard talking and rough."

"Someone who doesn't complain all the time and who thinks about my problems sometimes instead of just her own."

"You really know that she means it when she says she loves you."

The chapters immediately following will deal with the philosophy expressed by *Playboy* magazine and will also compare that philosophy of woman and life with the Christian and Jewish traditions. As you read the remarks printed here and make your own comments, you might keep thinking ahead. How does what is said here compare with what other people and publications are saying today about sex and women and people? What do you think makes a woman truly attractive? What role do you think women should have in relation to men? Do you think being a Christian should have anything to do with how men view women and with how women view men?

What Does a Woman Look For?

Just as a group of high school boys were asked to write down what they look for in women and what makes women attractive to them, a group of high school girls were asked to do the same about men. Below is what they had to say about the traits, the personality, the appearance, and the role they look for in men. The girls seemed to know better than the boys what they wanted and looked for, or at least they talked about it more readily. It would be rather easy to draw up a list of attractive qualities from what they said they looked for in a man. Some of the most basic qualities of the human being—both enduring and endearing—are in the comments. Some of them, like respect for others, understanding, gentleness, strength, are repeated again and again. Is it possible that what basically makes people truly human and attractive to each other are qualities of "person," even before they are qualities of either sex in some special way?

"A man to me is powerful, someone who can respect you. He is able to take over, when the going gets rough. A man should wear a nice haircut. I feel a man should show his head. Most of my boyfriends have a nice haircut."

"I think a man should treat you like a lady.

26

To me that is the most important. Because I think a man should respect you."

"I think it's his understanding for things I do or say."

"A man is a man if he's strong, protective, understanding, smart. If he respects you and cares for you he sticks up for his rights and yours; he treats you like a lady. It's hard to say because my ideas always change. I think he has to care about you, himself, and those around you."

"Aggressiveness, when he knows how to control his temper and emotions when I cry, or to know how and when to express emotion. He takes what's coming to him. He doesn't always run from work. He can get serious and talk with a girl and understand. He knows how to be strong but emotional too. It's underneath that counts."

"A man is a guy who has respect for women. He's strong in his body and his mind. He stands up for what he believes in. He's understanding and gentle and thinks of others before himself. He respects the ideas, opinions and wishes of others. He accepts you for what you are."

"A man is a man when he shows consideration for both himself and others. He must also be masculine, not a feminine type. I think he should never run away from a fight, and he should defend his girl's honor. (Very few do this anymore.) If another guy puts down your girl, you should knock him flat! A guy should be noble and gallant. (Old-fashioned words, and *very* ancient actions!) You never (almost) see this type of guy anymore. (He's extinct.) He should look deeper than a girl's physical attraction and he should sense her feeling and her inner self. The same goes for his male friends. Look deeper than the surface."

"A man is a man if he has respect for all people. He must also be intelligent and very mature. He should dress like a man. I think a man should have a good job too. I think a man's appearance makes a man too. He should have a lot of courage. He should be a good leader. He must be experienced. I think a man should be able to face his problems."

"A man doesn't just have to be good-looking. He has to be kind, courteous, thoughtful and he has to do thoughtful things for a girl. If he's cute and isn't thoughtful, he's not the guy for me. Sometimes his looks may attract me, but the real thing I care about is thoughtfulness. Most important of all, he has to respect me."

"A man who makes his own decisions and acts mature no matter who he's with is my kind. A man who loves me for what I am and who respects himself and me is what I'm after."

"In order to be a man, I think you need to act like a gentleman. Smoking, drinking and taking drugs to a great extent is a sign of weakness. He needs a crutch. Always getting into fights — to prove he is a man, that's weakness too. Knowing how to act around people and knowing how to treat a female is being a man. A man has to have gentleness too. Not always the hard role. A sweet, gentle personality. To be able to understand."

Once again, you may have some reactions to what you have just read. Many of the girls have stressed being accepted as a person and being loved for what they are instead of for what they look like.

They seem to demand character in men, and their expectations are in line both with the Christian viewpoint and with psychological good health.

What's your reaction...

Do you think the girls in this chapter have fully summed up the Christian viewpoint towards men?

What role do you think men should have in relation to women?

What do you think makes a man attractive as a man?

What do you think makes a girl attractive as a girl, or a woman attractive as a woman?

A SEXY ERA

4.

Some time ago the campaign for truth in packaging was rolling in high gear. The idea, of course, was that the customer should know exactly what he is paying for whenever he buys something in a package. It was a hard fight to get truth in packaging. It certainly was not a hard fight to get sex in packaging.

We do have sex in packaging. It was hardly even a campaign. It just became a matter of fact. As a matter of fact, we have sex in thinking, sex in entertainment, sex in the pursuit of happiness. We have sex coming out of every nook and cranny of our civilization. Living in a sexy era changes the approach to dating and marriage. At least it is a big consideration.

Sex in Packaging

Did you ever stop to think how many things you buy each week in packages? Your records come in albums, your cigarettes (if you have begun, or have not yet quit the nasty habit) come in boxes and cartons, your pop and beer come in bottles, your toothpaste comes in tubes, even your friends come in packages. Everything is wrapped, boxed, crated, presented, and then opened. The wrappings are the key to selling and sex is the key to wrapping.

Vance Packard wrote a book some years back in which he explained how human motivations are carefully studied by advertisers so they will know how to make their products appealing. In *The Hidden Persuaders* he asserted that sex is seen as one of *the* big motives. See if this isn't the truth. Just count all the girls and women you see in advertising during the next 24 hours; just count how many products use a picture of bare

31

flesh on the package; observe how many products are supposed to make you "attractive." For that matter, make a list of how many products you know for a fact are specifically sex-related products. The bra has become, next to Coca-Cola, America's most famous product. It is the symbol of our age.

Sex in Thinking

When we surround ourselves with sex symbols and sex reminders it is only a matter of time until our thinking becomes more and more sex-oriented. Probably a young man or woman thinks about sex more or less constantly anyway, once the drive to date and marry starts to take effect. Probably we wouldn't need any reminders that there is an opposite sex around. But just count how many reminders about the opposite sex will come your way before you go to sleep tonight.

The easiest way to remind someone about sex is to keep visual images of sex plastered all over everything they look at. Turn on TV, and in the space of one hour observe how many times a woman is shown undressing, being undressed, being kissed, kissing, arousing a man, or being pursued by an aroused man or men. Observe how many times the man is presented as the male, hunting women, bowling a woman over with his irresistible looks or physique or brutality or secret personality. Notice how many billboards do the same thing. Look at the movie page in today's paper and see if in fact you are not holding in your hands a huge collage on the sex theme.

Sex Is a Medium

Any philosopher can tell you sex is a medium. Sex is a way of communicating; a very easy, fast, well-understood way of communicating. The big temptation is to overuse the medium, especially when the medium is so naturally interesting and intriguing. The big danger is that we will start to evaluate things in terms of the medium through which they are presented. Given a dominant medium, our evaluation is likely to be weighted the same way. That is why the worth of a girl is likely to be weighted toward a consideration of her figure, of her sexiness, and of her romantic appeal. That is why the worth of a man tends to be weighted by whether or not he "turns people on." When this starts to happen, we start to underplay our own strong points in order to be noticed and valued. We start to fit the role and the image which the medium demands in order to present ourselves. Instead of being ourselves and looking for the real person in others, we begin to project a sex image and to look for the same in others. We get hooked on sex in packaging, whether she's a movie star, a prostitute, or our girlfriend. We get hooked on sex in packaging, whether he's a band leader, a tough guy, or just someone who's cool.

Sex Equals . . .

Sex obviously equals pleasure. So strong is this message today that anyone who doesn't experience, crave and expect sexual pleasure is taken to be some kind of odd species indeed. What it comes down to is a growing conviction and concern with sex and the things sex is supposed to bring. Originally, sex was a symbol for happiness. Among the Jews of the Old Testament, for example, sex was a symbol for life, and life was a symbol for happiness and eternal life. The unmarried man or woman was a tragedy. Not to be married meant not to be loved. It meant no children to be remembered by. It meant poverty and the end of the family name. It was a curse.

In our time, the big curse has changed. Today the curse is being left out sexually. It's not supposed to matter whether or not we marry. It just matters how we are doing with our sex life. To be left out sexually is supposed to mean trouble. The fear is that we will be tried and found wanting sexually. Sex is supposed to equal pleasure, peace, love, fulfillment, happiness.

What do you think?

Sex Is Good

Sex is more than good, it is great. In fact, it is one of the single greatest blessings God has bestowed upon us as people. It is one of the great joys of being human. Sex makes a man and a woman beautiful.

We do an awful lot of talking about sex, but not very much thinking. Just think, for example, of the many people who say many things about sex without thinking. For example:

People say sex is dirty. They don't stop to think that we were all born because of sex, and that our mothers and fathers were able to raise us because of love, which is a very sexual thing.

People say that teenagers are all sex crazy. They don't stop to think that the reason might be that teenagers are discovering the joy and thrill of being interested in someone else.

People say that sex is a big temptation. They don't realize that the reason sex is so tempting is because it is so good and so beautiful. Only attractive things can attract. We should be tempted toward good and beautiful things, people and activities.

People say sex takes us away from God. This is pure nonsense. Pleasure is not anti-God. Pleasure and delight, as even the book of Genesis points out, are man's prerogative, special gifts from God.

People say sex must be controlled. They mean that if sex isn't controlled, we will commit sin. We ought to be much more afraid of falling into sins of hate and indifference against people, although some people don't consider these atrocities as sin. We have made a fetish of nit-picking for sin when love relationships are involved, and then we have tried to live by this selective morality. There are sins with sex because there are sins against people, not because sex is bad, because it isn't.

People say sex shouldn't be talked about. That's because they don't know what we are talking about.

People say sex is a separate category, a special topic for morality, a special worry, something kids need instruction in and advice about. They don't stop to think that sex could never be a separate consideration. Sex means personality, sex means identity, sex means creativity. Sex means happiness and adventure. Sex, in a word, keeps us alive and makes life an adventure.

There are people in the English-speaking cultures who do not approve of too much talk about sex. There are many more who think our sexual morality is breaking down. They point to the high divorce rates and to the many other sex crimes, and they wonder out loud if perhaps religious leaders ought to be preaching the sinfulness of sexuality a little more firmly. Their concern is natural. The English-speaking cultures of the world have always had their share of conservatism toward sex.

For a long time many, many Christians' viewed sexuality as temptation and as a source of shame and guilt, something not even to be mentioned. Anything human was impure and somehow dirty. The official teaching of the Church, too, for a long time reflected a great fear of sex and counseled restraint and caution as the prevailing attitude that should characterize a Christian's behavior in the face of strong temptation.

It is only natural, then, that many people today would decide that new attitudes and deeper insights into the whole question of sex are responsible for the change in behavior and dress that characterizes our era. But this viewpoint, like all other viewpoints involving the

religious perspective, must look back to
revelation.

The Scriptural Heritage

In the Old Testament, sex is considered a
gift, not a curse. Because of sex, we are fruitful.
Children are a blessing, and wedded love is
revealed as the greatest human happiness. Love
itself is considered as a living revelation and
reminder of God's love. Sterility, whether
physical or mental, is considered the equivalent
of death or a curse, one of the worst things that
could befall a man or woman.

The New Testament continues to build on
the attitudes of the Old Testament writers. St.
Paul points out that marriage is *the* sign of God's
love for the Church, his bride.

Our Lord himself became man, teaching by
his action once and for all that the human body
is good, not evil. Good in all its parts and in all
its functions. So good that he likens his Church
to a body, calling it his body, calling it his bride.

In the true Jewish and Christian traditions,
sex has always been good, because it serves love,
which is from God. People are of great value for
a Christian because they are of great value for
Christ who loves us all. When sex serves people
and adds to their love and happiness, sex is
Christian. To say that sex is great is to say just
about everything that can be said. Sex is great!

Comments Please...

Do you think pornography has gone too far today?

If you were a legislator, what kind of laws would you make concerning movies, magazines, and entertainment?

What impressions do you think a ten-year-old boy or girl has today in our country concerning marriage?

Do you think the country has changed much in its sexual attitudes since the time your parents were married?

PLAYBOYS
AND
CHRISTIANS

5.

Everyone knows about *Playboy* magazine. Everyone knows about the philosophy which Hugh Hefner, publisher of *Playboy* magazine and founder of the clubs, has been proposing. Or does everybody know? Hugh Hefner is not a lecherous old man and his philosophy is not a matter of nudity and naughty entertainment. His philosophy is neither crude nor naive. It is the philosophy by which millions and millions of Americans live, and it is a philosophy which is spreading.

Playboy Philosophy

Some things are definitely in and some things are definitely out in the Playboy philosophy:

— the girl with a big chest is in.
— sex appeal is in, whether it's fair skin and lots of exposure in a woman or muscles, suavity, good looks, and a spirit of adventure in a man.
— money is in.
— fun is in.
— good clothes and smooth styles are in.
— freedom and shedding of clothes and moral freedom are in.
— sexual intercourse is a high value because it brings pleasure.
— spontaneity toward the other sex is in.
— prudishness is out.
— morals are a fiction.
— honesty is old-fashioned.
— responsibility is to be avoided.
— squares are out for good.
— pregnancy is out.
— children are something not to get stuck

with, at least not while you are young.
— marriage is out, at least for people who
want fun.
— work is only a necessity.
— cars, vacations, fun, pleasure, friends
are in.

Values

The old Puritan morals are definitely frowned upon in Playboy philosophy. The restrictions which used to be placed on sexual behavior, and even on marriage, are pretty well knocked down in this type of thinking. The values here are pleasure, beauty, freedom, personal development, and the good life. Health and appearance, image, and importance are some things to be sought. Youth is the great value, old age the enemy.

If you happen to be crippled or old, poor or clumsy, scrupulous or religious, you don't fit. If you are a child or a woman with a poor build, you are in trouble. If you are obese or scrawny, full of skin disfiguration or sick, you are no longer in. In fact, you are out. You've had it.

It would be unfair to condemn Playboy philosophy on all counts, because there is a lot of truth in what is being said. For example, what is wrong with stressing sexual beauty and attractiveness? These are certainly values, and sex is certainly a great pleasure and a thing of deep satisfaction. After all, the whole world is permeated with sexuality. Sex makes things grow, makes things attractive, makes life sparkle, makes a woman more a woman and a man more a man.

Again, what is wrong with stressing pleasure? Certainly pleasure is good and money is good and there is nothing at all bad about searching after the things which bring pleasure, nothing at all bad about wanting to make money and spend money and enjoy the good life. The good life wouldn't be called the good life if it were something evil, something dangerous, something awful or deceitful. So *Playboy* magazine is raising a stress that has not often been raised before in this country. The philosophy is pointing especially to youth and to beautiful women and to the beauty of sex, saying how good and how wonderful they are.

What is underplayed in Playboy philosophy is something that many of us are made aware of just by being alive. That is, the importance of personality, and of all people. Most of us come from families and friends who are not noted for youth, money, beauty, or freedom. Our fathers are generally not playboys and they are certainly not bachelors. Our brothers and sisters are usually not rich. Our mothers for the most part have given up much of their figure and much of their youth on our account. We have all known sickness and sorrow, we have all loved people for things that Playboy philosophy discards.

There are two sides to life. There is the side Playboy philosophy stresses, the beautiful flashy, exciting, attractive side. Then there is the deep, sincere, valuable-underneath part of life. That's the side Christianity has always stressed.

Christian Philosophy

Christian philosophy has its roots in the Jewish experience and wisdom. This is, in the main, the wisdom of the Old Testament and the reflection upon life found in the New Testament and in the Jewish tradition. The Old Testament was 12 centuries in the making. Adding to this the two centuries of experience which went into the writing of the New Testament, we find in the Bible the reflections and wisdom gained by God's people during a 14-century span of history. What it took people 14 centuries to realize is ours for the reading, if we care to examine the Bible and notice what is being said.

The Person Is In

From the very first chapter of Genesis to the very last chapter of the Apocalypse, we find a steady, unwavering emphasis upon the person as a central value in life for anyone who wishes to be a member of God's people. So important is the person in God's eyes that he will allow them to sin against himself rather than violate the sacredness of their freedom. So important are people to God that he cannot hate them, even when they hate him and each other. People are so important to God that he sees in them a reflection of himself and loves each person he makes forever.

In the eyes of the prophets, people are so important as individuals that each man must make a personal choice to be a member of the nation. Each man must covenant with God. Every person counts. When one person sins he must be held accountable, just as the merit of each person must be honored and respected. So important are people that the nation exists to serve people, rather than people existing to serve the nation.

There is a steady push, too, to make men realize that women are their equals. In the early Jewish history, women were considered only barely human. The stress in Genesis upon the woman's part in sin was an attempt to show the equality of women, even in such things as sin and love. To make a woman half responsible for the first sin was the equivalent of saying she counted, too, even in bad things. This idea in Genesis soon developed into an outright condemnation of the idea that women were mere playthings, that a man could have many wives, and that a man could divorce a woman. By insisting that men marry, and by making them go through the divorce courts in order to put a woman away, the idea was developed that every person counted. By the time of Christ the respect and value of each person were stressed to the point of making marriage a permanent commitment, one of his most explicit teachings.

The same type of development occurs in regard to slaves and children. Gradually God's people were made to realize that even their slaves had to be respected and that slavery was not a natural or desirable state for any human being. St. Paul concludes that the only type of slavery worthy of the name is slavery to God, which is what each of us should be involved in, but which God rejects. God has made us all free, with the dignity of being his heirs and adopted sons and daughters.

In our Christian tradition, then, it cannot be said too often that the person is "in" forever, with all of the implications involved. Slavery, racism, divorce, sexual abuse, insensitivity, disrespect for the helpless and weak, taking advantage of others, envy, quarrels, and all other crimes against the human person are "out." It's a tall order to make people the core of our values and the bedrock of our morality, but then it's a tall order to be a Christian.

Actions Are a Test of Love

For a Christian, actions will always speak louder than words. The picture of Christ dying silently on the cross shouts out to everyone looking on, for here was a man who gave his life for us. To imitate this man and to agree with this man means we at least will serve one another, as he indicated. It means none of us is too good to bow down to our neighbor and help him in need.

It means none of us is qualified to condemn our neighbor. It means when we love someone it's for good and not just for a time. It means we take our friendships seriously enough to make them permanent. It means we accept our husband or wife for what they are, and not as a plaything. It means not only that we refrain from exploiting people but that we go out of our way to get involved with all the people who come our way. It means we remember the sick and the ugly amongst us, the repulsive and the maimed, the helpless and the poor, the criminals and the insane, the unattractive and the depressed, the suffering and the dying people who fill this world. It means the basis for love is more than sexual attractiveness and physical beauty, more than money and gain, more than our own advantage.

In the Christian approach to things, the way we live is more important than the way we pray. The way we think is more important than the way we pretend to think. The way we act is more important than the things we promise. The way we treat other people is more important than the way we say other people should be treated. The way we *are* is most important of all.

Heaven is not for the pious-faced, holy-looking, prayer-mumbling, whitewashed, respectable well-wishers, but for the people who are like Christ. In the Christian tradition the children and the weak, the sufferers and the honest people are the ones who count most. People who really care about others usually end up looking just like Christ: friendless, homeless, dirty, despised, and often abused for their convictions. The Christian values people higher than the Playboy, and at least as high as himself. He is willing to stick to his values when the chips are down. He is no fly-by-night opportunist who leaves a trail of broken hearts, broken homes, and broken people behind him as he journeys through life.

In Christian philosophy, finally, what a man or woman *is* counts for more than what a man or woman looks like. What a man or woman *does* counts far more than what impression is made upon other people. The Christian is the person who makes a choice for people. That's where he finds God.

After reading that...

Do you think the Playboy philosophy and the Christian philosophy of love are compatible? In what respects?

Are women infact equal to men in our culture today? Should they be?

What is your reaction to the statement, "The Christian is the person who makes a choice for people. That's where he finds God?"

Do you think it is true that the way we live is more important than the way we pray? Would a Playboy agree with such a statement?

THIS HEART WAS MADE FOR LOVING...

6.

What is love? Nobody knows what romantic love is. Everybody knows when someone is in love, and everybody wants to be in love. But love defies explanation. Psychologists can describe romantic love as mutual attraction, mutual pre-occupation with the person we love. But words fail to describe our feelings and our condition. Shakespeare wrote that love is a many-splen-dored thing. Nobody quarrels with that.

Love, of course, covers more things than romantic love. It includes all our relationships with people and with the world. For Gandhi, love meant he had to be hungry when his brother humans were hungry. For Martin Luther King, love meant he could not accept respectability or status until his brothers and sisters were accepted everywhere in America. For Malcolm X, love meant risking death for the sake of justice. For Jesus, love meant dying so that we could live. For Paul, love meant the burning, driving mission to spread the good news of the redemption. What Paul said of love characterizes true love, whether it be romantic or otherwise:

Love is kind.
Love is patient.
Love believes all things.
Love hopes all things.
Love bears all things.
Love does not envy, is not puffed up, seeks not its own.

The few things any of us knows about love apply all the time, but especially when we are in love. We know, for example, that love is beauti-ful, whatever beautiful is. We know that love is so beautiful we just wish it would never end. We know, too, that love is ecstasy. It's so exciting that we don't seem to need sleep when we are in love. We aren't hungry. Our energy level goes higher and higher. Life looks rosy. No problem looks too big. Everything is fine. Love is so exciting that the time we spend with the person we love seems to fly by in a rush. Hours seem like minutes.

The urge for union and unity which accompanies love often includes a biological urge and emotional urge for union and possession. Eventually, love has to go deeper than urges for union. Eventually, people in love must *achieve* union at all levels. People who have loved for a long time begin to think alike and to feel the same emotions. The romantic qualities of love are indeed temporary when compared with this level of love where the very existence of two people begins to melt into one full existence.

This sharing of existence is the element common to all love. It was the outstanding characteristic of the prophets, who suffered and endured exile and death with their people. It was the most notable characteristic of the rabbis, ministers, and priests who died in the extermination camps of Germany and who endured captivity in the prisoner-of-war camps. It is this same quality, this sharing of existence, which leads mothers and fathers to unbelievable heights of heroism for their children and for each other when war strikes. It is the same force which holds a farmer to the land he loves even when his crops bring little or no money. It is the force which moves an unwed mother to keep her child and which brings a divorced father back to see his children.

What is love? No, the question can be posed only in terms of people. Love cannot exist as a "thing" or a "what." It is a quality of being, a dimension of living, a facet of personhood.

Nobody knows what love is until it comes, and then he is really confused. When love is gone and the flame is out, we still can't say what happened. All we seem to be able to say for sure is that for those who fall in love and stay in love, wisdom begins to dawn. Such people know what they know, and they are happy. Lovers understand all things and believe all things and endure everything.

Beauty: What Is It?

Beauty for some people is the stars. It is the sun coming up over a calm lake, whitecaps breaking under a sailboat, a tree covered with snow. These things are all physical in character but they are perfect, very appealing, extremely soothing. The idea of physical perfection as beauty is as old as the Greeks.

For the Greeks, the beauty in line and form inspired temples and statues, poems and sculpture of incredible perfection. The beauty of the human body was also noted by them, for in the human body they saw line and figure, curve and symmetry which seemed to be the epitome of all nature's work. It is from the Greeks that we inherit our ideas about what kind of figure makes a woman beautiful, and the profile that is supposed to be sexy is basically the Greek notion that the ideal profile is one of beautiful line broken by curves. For the man, the body beautiful combines line and curve with strength and grace.

For the existential philosophers, beauty rests not in appearance of the body but in the personality. Not everyone is beautiful for the existentialists, because, they point out, people can often be full of hate and bitterness inside. Inside we can be dwarfs, turned in upon ourselves, undeveloped in the qualities that make for a healthy personality. We can be selfish, afraid, alone. For the existentialists, the beauty of human beings has nothing to do with their physical appearance but with their qualities of existence, their inner beings, their personality and their mind.

For the Christian, all persons are beautiful just because they are persons. Every creature is beautiful simply because it exists, but even more so a human creature, because human creatures are endowed with intellectual and emotional qualities of existence which exceed those of any other creature and which last forever.

Not everyone is agreed that people are more beautiful than things. It may well be, for example, that some art collectors think certain paintings the highest beauty ever achieved by man. Others may think a perfectly cut diamond is far more beautiful than even a woman's eyes. Others may think a certain poem is the ultimate in beauty. Still others may see beauty personified in sculpture or in nature.

Some philosophers have argued against most other notions of beauty by saying that beauty is actually in the eye of the beholder. It is not nature or a person or the poem or the statue that is beautiful; rather, we see these things, and in looking at them, we bestow beauty upon them, seeing them as beautiful. It's like the saint who looks at the leper and sees him as beautiful. What these philosophers suggest is that no matter what we look at, we are constantly endowing things with beauty or lack of beauty, because it is we who make the thing beautiful or not. The greatest example they point to is love, where the lovers see each other as far more beautiful than anyone else.

The Options

No matter what philosophy of beauty one accepts, we can all agree that whatever it is we see as beautiful, we are attracted to it. The art collector wants the prized picture, the nature lover tries to photograph nature's beauties and is always looking at them, the diamond lover buys diamonds. The same is true with people we see as beautiful. We want to be with them and we want to look at them and we think about them. That is why it is so important to decide what it is in people that constitutes real beauty. What we decide will determine the kind of love we will bestow upon one another. It will also determine the kind of people to whom we will be attracted.

Our options for seeing beauty in people are fairly clear. We may look for physical beauty, which in our culture is synonymous with sexual beauty. This would mean marrying the best-shaped girl with the prettiest face and figure or the best-built man with the thickest hair and finest clothes. Or we may go by personality, loving a person for what he or she is. We may then look for the kindest, most patient, smartest, or most understanding person we meet. We may marry on the basis of the inner qualities we find in someone of our acquaintance. Or we may say that since every person is beautiful, we will love the person who needs our love the most, choosing to love someone because he is a person, trying to see through to the fact that he is an existing human being who needs our love to grow and be happy.

What usually happens when falling in love is that physical beauty gets our attention first, and then gradually we begin to see the inner qualities of the person, and finally we offer our love. The pattern is usually one of enjoying or possessing at first and then gradually learning to give more and more until our love becomes a sharing of existence rather than an acquiring of a beautiful body or a beautiful mate.

The decision about beauty will have a great bearing on love, obviously, and it will have a great bearing upon our happiness. There is an old saying that beauty is more than skin deep, but such a saying has a deeper significance than many people care to admit. Where our hearts are will be determined by what we think is beautiful. And where our hearts are is where our love will be, too, for we will always seek union with what we love.

This Heart Was Made For Lovin'

Everybody loves a baby and every man loves the luscious blond. Are these two loves contradictory? Our culture has connected love to sex, so that nonsexual love is no longer thought of as love at all, but as a duty or a chore. Playboy philosophy, for example, as we have seen, would stress the importance of sexual games but would caution us not to get so involved that we end up married and with children to tie us down. It's not people we are advised to love but sexually exciting people. Our "love" is supposed to be selective and temporary and terribly exciting. It's not that playboys hate children. They like kids, but they hate the responsibility kids bring. It's not that they don't love a woman enough to marry her, but that they don't want to be tied down, to lose their freedom.

Christianity has always stressed the non-sexual aspects of love, in contrast to the Playboy philosophy. The Christian is traditionally supposed to view love as sacrifice, as something for the benefit of the loved one rather than for the benefit, pleasure, or satisfaction of the lover. Of course, without love for children, how would children survive? Without stable families based on stable marriages, how could any of us have grown up to be healthy and happy? Of course love involves responsibility.

Psychology presents still a third view of love, the view that we die as a person when we do not love, just as we die when we are not loved. A psychologist will generally be concerned to make sure we are loving, rather than worrying about how much love we are receiving. That is because any psychologist knows that we can't love anyone for very long without becoming lovable in their eyes. If we are loving in a healthy, steady manner, being loved will take care of itself. The relationships we strike up between people are the essential ingredient that will determine our own self-value and self-concept, and the key ingredient in our relationships is our own love, because that is the part of a relationship we can do something about.

Parts of the Picture

Are Christianity, Playboy philosophy and psychology as diametrically opposed as we sometimes think? Are these three notions of love so far apart? Do we have to choose one of the three as our philosophy of love? Or is it not possible that all three viewpoints about love express a part of the truth?

Certainly, for example, Christianity as taught has often tried to hide sex, and many twisted Christian thinkers have tried to condemn sex as sin and evil. Religion has not always publicized the beauty and freedom of sex, for in fact it has often tried to "scare" us away from even thinking about sex. *Playboy* magazine, on the other hand, has not exactly been the great friend of children and old people. It has made sexual attractiveness, rather than personality and character, the test of a person's worth. Old people and children are out of the picture because they have nothing to offer. And psychology has underplayed the reasons and motives for loving and being loved, making the whole matter very often self-survival or self-enhancement. Why not accept all three viewpoints balanced together? Christianity, Playboy philosophy, and psychology all have some good things to say about love, which together present a magnificent philosophy of love.

When we say "God is Love," we utter a phrase we cannot understand. God's love is too deep, has too many dimensions to ever fully be captured. The same is true when we say to another human being "I love you." The love of another person is too deep to deserve or to understand. We can no more understand that other person's love than we can understand the love we give him.

Love does make the world go around and around, and it should make us go around and around, too. Our love will be unique. It can be beautiful. All our hearts were made for loving, but our love will be only the kind we choose.

Opinions Please...

What is your notion of beauty?

What do you think is the most beautiful thing in the world today?

If you had one billion dollars, what would you spend it on?

Do you think you are beautiful?

DATING

7.

When we were just tiny little things we cried to let people know we were hungry. We cried to let people know we were uncomfortable. Mother came running with food, with clean diapers, with water, with tenderness and affection. We soon discovered that the world was basically a pleasant place to be in because everybody took care of us. We didn't even have the awareness that we were different from the people and things around us.

As a baby, everything seemed to be part of us. After a few months we became aware of our fathers and of other people, too, but the awareness was simply an awareness of more people who would meet our needs. What little awareness we had, then, was egocentric. Everybody loved us. We needed do little more than demand at the top of our lungs.

Growing Up

By the time we were two years old, it finally began to dawn on us that other people and objects were different from ourselves. We finally began to realize that we were different from other things. We began to demand things not just from the world at large, but from specific people. By the time we were two we began to make our own decisions about what we would do next. This is when other people became interesting. Even though we played with other two-year-olds, we really didn't play *with* them but *next* to them. We wouldn't share anything with anybody, but at least we liked to have other people around not to share things with.

When we were three years old we could use two shovels and only one pail and still not hit the three-year-old who was sharing our sandbox. It was important to us that we please our mothers and fathers. Of course we tried to please them in some unusual kinds of ways, like smearing butter on the icebox and pouring milk all over the table and floor. By the time we were three years old, we were great big grown-up persons who could talk! By the time we were five, we could enjoy groups of children! Of course the groups were really small mobs and we exerted no leadership whatever. Much of our time was spent arguing, but we enjoyed being in the small group and we were able to understand the justice of elementary sharing and courtesy.

Other crucial developments in our lifetime included the first gang stage we went through near the end of third grade. We actually began to make real friends. We established ourselves as a boy or girl by associating mostly with other boys or girls. When we really wanted to get a boy all "shook" at this age, we just called him a girl. We felt much antagonism toward the opposite sex because they were a real pain.

By the time we were 13 or 14 we started associating with people of the other sex in large groups. At times we would go to the same parties, even though boys stayed near the wall on one side and girls ended up on their side of the room for most of the dance or party. We no longer ignored the opposite sex; in fact, we were very much aware of other people, especially people of the opposite sex. It was here that the last stage of real boy-girl relationships began, because it was here that dating began. Because of our dating, we learned how to establish ourselves as a male or female and to see someone of the opposite sex in their complementary role. We began to grow in love and we are still growing.

Encounter and Growth

Two things happen in every date: We meet somebody and we grow. Dating is fun because of the people we date. It's fun because it is basically sexually oriented exploration. When we date a boy or girl, we are trying to find out who they are and what they are like. We are trying to get to know them better and like them better. We are trying to relate to them at a more sophisticated level than we ever did before; we are trying to mean something to them and they are starting to mean something to us. The fact of the matter is that it takes a lot of practice before we can mean much to our friends, and it takes a lot of growth before we can even begin to love them except for the pleasure they bring us.

Maturing

To begin to date is to begin getting control of our personalities. This, of course, is a major step in the process of maturation that began when we were born and that will end when we die. It is the major step, the most important step in our personality development, for *if it does not occur, we will be doomed to exist basically alone for the rest of our lives.* It is also the crucial step for other people too, because the way we develop during the dating stage of our life will determine how we will treat our future husband or wife and how we will treat other people.

Our social graces and our emotional development at this time will make us the kind of person someone else is going to have to live with for the remainder of his life. Obviously,

62

too, our dating experiences will lead us to explore the possible chances for finding the one person we will love above all others and eventually marry. Without the dating experiences we will neither meet enough people nor learn all we need to learn about relating to other people. With a good dating experience behind us, we will find ourselves ready and willing to marry or to live as responsible, loving social beings in some other state of life.

Dating is both natural and necessary. It is so much fun that most people wonder about the morality of it, using the logic that anything that much fun can't possibly be OK. But dating is good, natural, necessary. It is part of our development and it is certainly a wonderful part of life. The question dating raises is the great question of life: What are other people worth and how shall I relate to them?

Dating Morality

Dating morality, though usually a big concern, is no different from any other morality. Our values determine our morality, and for the Christian, people are a value. This means, then, that in order to know what is right and wrong on a date we must consider what is good for our partner on the date and they must consider what is good for us.

The usual questions concerning dating morality are what about petting, what about necking, and what about French kissing? Are they wrong? Why are they wrong? How far can a person go without serious sin?

The answer to these questions lies in realizing that sex is more than physical intercourse. Sex is a display and an assurance of love. It includes kissing, petting, snuggling, holding hands, and even thinking. The entire date is a sexual experience. Friendship between a man and woman is sexual by nature. The deeper our love for one another, the more we will want sexual manifestation and assurance of love. So the question becomes, what does love demand?

If a man goes all the way with a woman who is not his wife, has he loved her or hated her? If either of them is married, of course, there is adultery. But suppose neither is married. For the man to have sexual intercourse with a woman to whom he is not totally committed is, among other things, to expose her to the insecurity and fear of losing him.

It will not be settled "where she stands with him." The same is true for the man. Emotionally, he may be assured of holding her as long as he wants, which is to admit he is a tyrant. Or he may be uncertain of her, which means he is just as insecure as she is. In either case, the man and the woman are saying, in so many words, that they are afraid to take a permanent chance on each other, that they would prefer to stay clear of "entanglements," to hold onto their freedom, to remain open to the possibility of a love relationship with someone else in the future. The whole relationship amounts to nothing else than the adolescent stage of dating as an exploration of possible life mates. The only added element is that in this case the exploration centers more on possible bed mates.

Signs of Love

No sign expresses love in our culture better than kissing. That's why kissing is so exciting. It is truly an experience to kiss, for the kiss speaks of affection and care. To kiss someone on a date without meaning it is already a mockery. It is saying something which is not true. To kiss for the pleasure without meaning the kiss is to use the person we kiss as an instrument of satisfaction. Any sexual act can be approached for the pleasure it brings, which pleasure is good. But if the pleasure of sex is at the expense of another person, we have done an evil thing. Just as sex and pleasure go together, so do sex and love go together. To love someone without security and permanence and sincerity is to deceive and use. Such irresponsibility attacks both our victim and the sacredness of sex itself, for it amounts to a serious abuse of man's happiest gift, that of love.

To portray God as begrudging us pleasure or counting sexual pleasure as sin is blasphemy. There is nothing wrong with pleasure, or it wouldn't be pleasure. As Christians, we do not go about weighing each ounce of pleasure, sexual or otherwise, to see how much sin is involved. We affirm pleasure to be beautiful and good.

What we do concern ourselves with, however, is our orientation. Are we people-oriented or pleasure-oriented? The Christian is people-oriented first and foremost, for people are of the greatest value. People are always worth more than the pleasure they bring. People's feelings are the main concern.

Love is more important than sex, and people are more important than pleasure. This is our orientation as Christians and this is the basic value priority upon which our morality rests. For the Christian, this is the only way to approach God or others with dignity and self-respect, for we are free men to the spirit, not slaves to our flesh.

As a Christian...

Do you agree with the statement:
   "To begin to date is to begin getting
control of our personalities"?

Do you agree that if a person does
not date during the teenage years
   they are doomed to be basically
   alone for the rest of their lives?

Do you think premarital
   intercourse is a betrayal?

If you were a parent would you
think premarital intercourse
   is wrong?

Perhaps the most frequently asked question about love and about sex comes out to be some form of "What is right and what is wrong?" We live in a culture where morality is a matter of key concern, a culture where the moral concerns differ drastically between the older and younger generations. For all the talking and arguing we do about morality, there is relatively little knowledge about morality. Oddly enough, we are more confused about love morality than about morality in any other area, and yet love is something about which we all know a great deal.

Moral Values

Morality begins with moral judgment. Simply speaking, a moral judgment is nothing more or less than a judgment that some action is a good action or a bad action or one that lies somewhere between good and bad, depending upon circumstances. Because such judgments cannot be made without values, values become a consideration, and in fact, the key consideration in making moral judgments.

We all know there is an almost unlimited variety of values available to us as human beings. What we seldom realize is the way values work once they become our values. Suppose, for example, that money becomes our value. Because money is important to us, anything which loses us money is bad and anything which makes us money is good. If we value money more than anything else, then anything which loses us money is the greatest evil for us, and anything which makes us money is always good.

We have all heard of people whose morality rests precisely on money as the strongest value.

They are the sort of people who would rather cheat a starving family than give up a few pennies. They are the sort of people who would rather sell war material, even to the enemy, than lose a little business. They are the sort of people who will do anything for money, even if it means other humans will suffer and die.

Values Change and Mix

Nobody builds their morality on only one value, and nobody can keep their values from changing. Even if money is the overriding value, for example, staying alive is also a value. So are health and happiness. So are friends. So are being loved and being important.

No matter what our values happen to be, they are likely to change and develop. Right now, for example, you probably consider such things as being appreciated, being loved, being successful and being accepted as high priorities. But later on you may place the welfare of your husband or wife and the health of your children at the top of your list. Later still you may want nothing more than to be able to get away from your friends and be able to retire. Every person operates on a different value structure, and therefore each of us works on a slightly different morality.

Love Morality

In the Christian context, the basic values are constant, including such things as love, life, justice, truth, purity, courage, freedom, people, and God. As Our Lord himself pointed out over and over, love is the most basic value for one who thinks with him. Love pretty much sums up most of the other laws and commandments in the Christian tradition.

In our lives, love has different dimensions, depending upon who we are and where we are. And so love morality has many possible dimensions. But once love becomes the most important thing in our life, we will tend to act out of love, and when we act out of love we can't be wrong.

This is the first thing about love morality that is crystal clear: Love is never wrong if it is really love. If we are Christian, love is our supreme value. Love takes many forms and sometimes we are fooled into false love. Sometimes our love leads us to mistakes. That's when we start to learn. That's what growing up is all about. When it's all over, we will find out that's what life is all about—all about love and loving and being loved.

Sex and Morality

Two points serve as the basis for any discussion of sex morality. The first is that sex is a way of expressing love. Sex includes dating and mating, kissing and dreaming, falling in love and falling out of love. Sex covers all the relationships between us and the opposite sex. If love is the basic moral value, then sex is regulated in terms of this basic value, and it is regulated *by us*. We use sex in light of our values, chief among which is love. When sex serves love it is good, and when sex works against love it is evil. The judgment has to be made by us because love is our value. That brings the discussion to the second point, conscience.

Conscience always seeks the good. Conscience is the ability to make a practical judgment for myself about what I am going to do or not going to do. When we start talking about the morality of sex behavior and sexual desire, we are talking about the decisions we are faced with. We are talking about the stuff that will keep our conscience "hopping" for a long time, maybe for the rest of our life. Conscience seeks not only the good, but the best for us and for others. Conscience is the ability we have to take morality out of the abstract choice of values and put it into the actual world of our actions and situations.

What About My Sex Life?

In the Christian tradition, as we have seen, the only adequate word for sex, as for love, is "great." Sex is God's gift to mankind, totally good, totally beautiful, totally enjoyable. In this respect Playboy philosophy is correct. This means that a naked woman is totally beautiful. This means that being naked for a man or for a woman means to display beauty and invite sexual response to beauty. This means that the human sexual experience is one of the greatest, deepest, most meaningful experiences available to us as people. A Christian accepts, therefore, as true, the following working principles:

— *love is great.*
— *sex is great.*
— *woman is beautiful, even more attractive when exposed in her naked beauty.*
— *the body is good.*
— *dating, going steady, and getting serious about someone is wholly desirable and good.*

— relating to people in love and in sexual love is a great source of happiness.
— love demands that sexual love be couched in the permanent relationship of marriage because of the security and honesty such sexual relationships reveal and demand.

What About Me?

After all these maxims are accepted as values, we have the makings of morality. The application of morality comes when we use our conscience to apply our values to our situation. Here is where the preaching starts, the moralizing sets in, the guilt and defensiveness and quarrels begin. It doesn't have to be this way, though, if we simply stick to our guns about love as the highest value. If we love somebody or want to be loved by somebody, we will insist that the love be responsible. Irresponsible love is not love at all, any more than irresponsible sex is an expression of love. For our own sake and for the sake of those whom we love, we will make responsibility the practical guide. That again is what conscience is: an assuming of responsibility for our actions.

Responsibility tells us we will not ask someone of the opposite sex to expose their full beauty by taking off their clothes unless we can respond to that beauty. Responsibility and love keep us from falling in love before we can provide for the person we love and before we are stable enough for them to relate to us permanently.

Responsibility and love mean different things, depending on whether we are dating, going steady, on a honeymoon, married with a family, or old married people. The love remains. The responsibility remains. But the circumstances and situations change. So does our judgment about what is best, what is good, what is bad, what is questionable. Naturally we want to do the best by the people we love, and naturally we want to love.

So what's the problem?

Christ has taught a great vision of love. For him, love is good, and it is always good, in all respects. For him, there is no right and wrong for love, no "rules" for love, no morality to be examined and followed when it comes to love. He explained what he meant by saying that love sums up the whole law and the prophets, too. Love God and love your neighbor, and all the laws will be taken care of, for they are just so many ways of spelling out how we ought to love. God is good. Love is from God and of God, and God is bound by no morality, for he is all good.

Where we need morality and where we are bound by the right and wrong is not in love but in our pursuit of love and in our quest for a mate. The right and wrong of sex and dating behavior are derived from the value of love and from our desire to love. If we waste our affection, if we make a mockery of union, if we make playthings of our friends and reduce mating to biological pleasure, we are hurting our chances for true human relationships. If we play at love and make a game out of affection, what can we hope for? If we treat our dates like objects, how can we hope to relate to them as people?

We will be happy when we love. Love is the real thing when it makes people bigger and when it leads us to be concerned for them. Love is authentic when it makes a mask unnecessary and

when it knocks down walls between people.
Love is beautiful when it destroys loneliness by
creating union.

Honestly Now . . .

What are your six top values?

Would you die for any of your values
rather than betray them? Which ones?

Do you know anyone whose actions
would indicate that money is their
number one value?

How much do circumstances affect
the rightness and wrongness of what
we do?

How much does our intention affect
the rightness and wrongness of
what we do?

Is morality absolute? In what
sense?

A TIME
FOR
MARRYING . . .

9.

When a baby gets up on the edge of the crib and looks out, we say the baby is curious and cute. When a teenager gets up on the edge of a situation and tries to find out who adults are, adults say he is prying and impertinent. Curiosity about other people and their personalities means we are filling out and growing. It characterizes sexual development, and indeed, human development. The fact of the matter is that people who are curious about others are usually puzzled about themselves, too, and that's why they check out how other people think.

Most of us have gone through or are going through this curiosity. Men have always been noted for their curiosity about what makes women do what they do and think what they think, and this curiosity eventually comes to be centered in one or two particular girls or women. This same curiosity strikes girls and women, and it gets to us all about the rest of our group as a whole. The curiosity, when it first comes, means we are concerned enough about other people to find out how they are authentic and real. It's another way of saying we want to be authentic and real, which is to be independent. The idea is to be worthwhile and valuable like other worthwhile and valuable people, but to be different at the same time. There is a pattern in this personality exploration which most of us are involved in, and the pattern can usually be seen in a time cycle.

Social Development Is Cyclical

Just about everything we do as humans can be observed in time and space, and our pattern of relating to other people is no exception. Our curiosity and exploration of other people's personalities occur in a fairly regular cycle. The cycle covers about a ten-year span for most people. It begins with the first mixed party and ends with the first or second child. By actual count and observation, it can be predicted that a boy or girl will be bringing their first or second baby home from the hospital ten years after their first mixed party.

When we were in grade school, boys and girls didn't start to get romantic until perhaps the seventh or eighth grade. It was hard to break the ice and a lot of us didn't want to break the ice with the opposite sex. But the ice broke with a dancing party or a skating party or a beach party, and once these started, it was only a matter of time until we found ourselves group dating.

Group dating doesn't last long. Before we know it, we are casual dating, and before long we are serious about someone, maybe even "pinned." It is only a matter of time before casual dating and social dating become romantic dating. The "field" gets narrow and before long somebody is getting seriously engaged or going all the way or getting married. The natural development seems to go from mild curiosity in the beginning to group socializing to individual romantic love, and then to really serious engagement or marriage. What the process represents is a growth from being self-centered to being in love, which is to be centered on someone else entirely and exclusively.

What's Best?

It is obviously a matter of debate just when the process of growing up and becoming an adult has finally been accomplished. For some of us, it never quite seems to be accomplished. Even more debatable is the question of when the first mixed parties should begin, because it is debatable when people should get married. If the first mixed parties begin when we are ten, we can plan on marrying at 20 or sooner. That means we are likely to be grandparents by the time we are 40.

Religion doesn't have any commandments that tell us when to start the pattern of our sexual and personal development which will culminate in adulthood. No one, as a matter of fact, can make this type of decision for us. So each person has to ask himself at what age he or she plans to marry and when he or she would like to be a parent. The answers to these questions come in the form of our decisions about our social and romantic life now.

Is He (She) the One for Me?

There are all kinds of ways to find the person we love, and as many different ways as there are people. Someone who feels he is ready for marriage may decide on the first date that this is the girl for him. Someone else might take years to decide. A girl in the marrying mood might meet the man for her before she knows what has happened. Other women become careful and delay; a few women can't decide between two or three men.

How do we know when Mr. or Miss Right has arrived? What makes a girl so different that she's the one, or a boy so different that he's the one? The first step in knowing who the right one is lies in knowing ourselves.

78

There are, of course, many different ways to judge maturity, but self-knowledge is common to all the definitions. We probably never really know entirely who we are, partly because who we are is always changing, and partly because we don't think very much about it. All of us have met people who are more mature at 20 than other people at 50; we know in our own group there are many levels of maturity, all of which in the end hinge on the amount of self-knowledge and self-honesty individuals possess.

Part of the excitement of high school comes because of the self-knowledge we are gaining. More than at any other time in life, high school years bring us face to face with ourselves. We are testing out our athletic and social skills; we are testing out our intelligence; we are testing our wits and our sensitivities; we are finding out where we fit in the world and how we impress people; we are finding out where our attractiveness and real worth are to be found. The truth of this comes home right after we leave school.

When all the dust has settled and we find ourselves out of school, the immensity of the high school experience starts to hit us. We start to find out how firm our convictions have become and how strongly we feel about such things as war and love and people and policy.

We all know couples who married during high school or right after high school, and we can just see the growth they are experiencing. Sometimes what happens to these couples is very similar to what happens to us, too. The last stage of growing up occurs and they wake up changed people. Their self-awareness and self-knowledge seem to jell, and suddenly they find themselves at odds with their partner. They simply cannot agree on key points because of who they are and who they have become. It's the same with us. Immediately after high school we will feel some friendships deepening and others breaking apart, because we are stronger-minded, more mature, more convinced people who stand for things and who know where we stand.

Marry in Haste, Repent at Leisure

Many very early marriages succeed, but it takes good luck and some great adjustments for them to last. The younger a man is, the stronger his urge to run with old buddies, to drink a little on the heavy side, to be away from home for a good time, to resent extra demands and hardships.

The younger the wife, the more she needs to keep track of her old friends, to do things with her friends, to resent children too soon, to feel oppressed by being cooped up in the same apartment or house for days on end, and to have an endless stream of advice beamed her way by older married women who look upon her as still a girl. A high school marriage is usually followed by the dating process.

During the dating process, people get to know one another better and better. But in the case of an early marriage, this occurs only after marriage. In the case of most young people, since this occurs before marriage, the people dated usually turn out to be not quite right. The same is true of most people who get married too early: They turn out to be not quite right for each other.

How to Find Out

One way to find out who is right for us and who isn't the one we want is to do a lot of talking. If all we can do on a date is go swimming or watch a show or be entertained, we really haven't found out very much. If we can't tell from our dates whether or not our partner wants a big family or a small family, whether he or she believes in baby-sitters or not, what our partner thinks about finances and value and careers, what makes for happiness, what he or she dreams about and how crises affect him or her, then we need to do more talking. Our partner needs to know all these things about us, too, and that means we have to share our self-knowledge more than we have ever done before.

Another way to decide whether or not we love somebody well enough to spend our whole life together is to start meeting important people such as parents, brothers and sisters, friends and people from whom our partner gets advice. When we begin to like the same people our partner likes, when we like to do the same things together, when we understand one another, when we can talk about anything without being phony, when we can practically read each other's minds and when we like what we are reading, we've found the right partner.

Until we are sure that we have matured to a point of stability, it isn't fair to commit ourselves to a partner for life. We can expect to change drastically, but we can't always expect the person who marries us to be able to adjust to our new personality developments and shifts of conviction.

Mating

Philosophers have always bemoaned the loneliness that men bring upon themselves. Which one of us can say loneliness is not something we dread, something we work all the time to avoid? Somehow loneliness always brings up the thought of death, for at the moment of death we are truly alone. The same philosophers who see death as the evil it is, tell us we are dying before our time when we succumb to loneliness.

People build wall after wall between themselves. We wear all sorts of masks. We wear a mask for our parents, a mask for our teachers, a mask for our friends, a mask for public, sometimes even a mask for our own conscience. As human beings, we so easily and quickly put on a mask that we cut ourselves off from one another without even knowing it. When we are not honest, it is impossible to share the existence of the people around us. We become lonely even in a crowd. The culture we live in seems to encourage loneliness, and the pressure of life forces us to it. Yet we know we were not meant for loneliness and we know it is ridiculous to be alone in life. The reason that loneliness is ridiculous? Because we can love and because we want to love.

Anyone who has ever been in love knows that loneliness is neither natural nor inevitable. In fact, it's not even a danger for lovers. Very few of us can deny that we are lovers at heart. The urge to mate is part of most men and women. Most of us have a built-in yearning to love one man or one woman on an exclusive basis, permanently. The reason is, again, a simple one:

Exclusive love is a way of sharing the existence of the person we love. It is a way to share our existence. It is the deepest and most beautiful relationship we could have, and part of its beauty is that we are happy when we share our existence, unhappy when we do not. To love is to be human, and to be truly human is to be happy.

What of this urge to mate? It is both biological and emotional. We do not want to be alone. We do not want to be without the specific affection of one person of the opposite sex. The urge to mate includes the urge to physical union, but it runs deeper than this. The urge to mate is the urge to be consumed by the person whose existence and esteem we share; it is the urge to be permanently united in life, and to never again be alone.

In Your Judgement...

Do you know anyone who married the wrong person? How can you tell?

Do you agree with the theory put forth here that ten years or sooner after the first mixed party you will be coming home with your first or second child?

At what age do you think people should begin dating?

Do you think there should be a legal age limit, below which marriage would not be allowed? What should that age be?

BEGINNINGS

10.

Ask any bride and she will tell you the week before the wedding is something you want to go through only once. The whirlwind of invitations, people you forgot to invite, bills to pay, menus to check, telephone calls, helpful relatives and last-minute arrangements are maddening. The last few days are a frantic round of showers, parties, worries, and people.

Everybody's emotions are flowing over. People begin to cry over the bride-to-be, friends begin to mock the man about to be captured by a marriage license, parents give all sorts of help you wish they didn't, and you generally get the jitters about the whole thing.

If for no other reason than peace, the day after the wedding is heaven itself. It takes all of one day to know getting married was a very good idea. After one day the wife or husband is far more lovable than we had ever hoped they could be. The jitters go away and happiness sets in. That's why honeymoons are so important: so we can enjoy our happiness with each other and not have all sorts of distractions. It's one of the happiest times in life.

Marriage Sex

Sex in marriage begins during the honeymoon, but so does the realization that from now on sex will be an integrated part of our experience. From now on it isn't necessary to get a date with the person we love; we don't have to wonder and worry about "moral" behavior and about controlling every move we make, for fear of committing sin. Our love grows so fast that sex immediately becomes only an expression of love, part of the much bigger experience of belonging to someone forever, someone who loves us and is happy to be with us.

The honeymoon is a magnificent chance to grow in one another, one too good to let slip by. It is surely a taste of the ultimate. The most fantastic thing of all, though, is that love *just begins* on the honeymoon. It will deepen and grow so much that, periodically, married people can talk over the past few months and see how much their love has deepened. It will often seem as though the honeymoon was the springboard for a great and wonderful growth in love that just starts to spill over into more and more happiness.

Married Love

No one has ever been able to say what love is. People know when we are in love, and we know when someone else is in love, but it is hard to put into words what it all means. Love is a joyous embrace of everything, which makes it hard to describe. We are thrilled, and we feel a peaceful happiness just because the person we love exists. We want that person to live and love and be happy.

First love is exciting and thrilling. Honeymoon love is unbelievably beautiful because it is ecstasy to be continually near the one we love. Then, later, in the routine of daily life, our love grows quieter and deeper, much deeper than we believed possible.

Marriages fail, of course, when love fails. How does love fail? We have a curious characteristic as humans. While we are capable of knowing others deeply, we can often harbor resentments or half-formed hates until they build up a wall between ourselves and others. When we stop expressing ourselves and being open, the walls begin to choke off the love.

Mature persons can weather any storm, because they keep communicating. Immature persons can't or won't stay open to each other, and their love shrivels. Given communication, married love is ecstasy and mystical experience; the actual lovemaking becomes an indescribable joy. If there is no communication, married love becomes a pretext, and lovemaking becomes a source of shame.

For a man and wife, every act of married love is a deeply fruitful expression. It is a special time, a marvelously silent time, when, away from the worries, frustrations, and ceaseless labor of life, they concentrate their attention on the person they love most. It is a time of beautiful pleasure, a time in which the spiritual quality eventually surpasses and transcends the beautiful physical experience, a moment of growth.

Just as married love defies description, so too, the birth of a child as a creation of love becomes indescribable. A child is the priceless gift of unity. A child is life from love incarnate. In our children we live on, and our love lives on, for the child returns love for love while growing to the maturity of manhood or womanhood.

A Foretaste of Heaven

So deep and beautiful is it to have children, that for the Jews of old, marriage and children were the symbol of heaven. There was no higher happiness then, nor is there any higher happiness for us today. Marriage is still the symbol of heaven, and children are still the fruit and the embodiment of love. Married love and all that marriage involves is still the greatest revelation we have of God's love, of God's concern, and of life itself. Married love and children are a sharing in the life of God, for God is love. Love is the beginning and the end and all else besides.

We use many images to describe love. Love is like a river, running deeper and deeper, quiet on top, running strong underneath. Lack of love, or hate, is like a wall between two people, choking off love, dividing them. Real love is tested by storms, just as the test of a good ship is the storm. Strong love weathers the storm and proves itself. Love is fruitful, like the rich earth, bringing forth children that are the fruit of love and the harvest of happiness. Married love is like heaven, for it is the greatest human happiness on this earth and it foreshadows the happiness of heaven.

It is inevitable that we speak of love in images, because the description of love, like love itself, cannot be exhausted. It's like trying to find the bottom in a bottomless well. Love is like a diamond, with many facets and appealing aspects. Love is like fire, ever spreading and always re-kindling. Love is light in the darkness, as St. John noted. Love is like a spring, ever bubbling up fresh and full love. Married love, in a word, is a great sign and a great gift, both revealing and creating.

Those Important Two Years

We often speak of a husband and wife as being marriage partners, meaning they are in it together, they can only be happy if they work together, and so on. But the word "partner" is a poor word to use because of what being a partner suggests. Partners are what we find in business. Partners are people who enter into a mutually profitable business. Partnerships dissolve when they aren't working out. Partnerships suggest the cold, impersonal, efficient arrangements which gets things done in our society today. Certainly married couples have to arrive at an understanding about hundreds of things in order to live together in harmony. Certainly they need to be efficient and to work together; but the adjustments two people make in marriage must be approached ever so delicately and ever so lovingly that they demand more than a partnership approach. It takes so much sensitivity to each other's feelings that the two people in marriage must be much more than partners. They must share one another's existence.

More Than Talking

The working values of two individual persons are never the same. Both persons in a marriage will inevitably have to do some bending, even when they don't want to bend and even when bending seems like a bad compromise. Of course we never give up values for anybody, but the form and shape of our values is something subject to modification, something that will often have to change in marriage. That is why talking is more than just talking in marriage.

There are bound to be crisis points in communication between married people — crisis points which must be expected. For most couples, many of these crisis points will occur early in marriage, before the first year of married life has gone by. When this happens, communication is absolutely vital. At this point, communication is more than talking. The temptation is to not talk things out, to not "rock the boat," to "drop it" and to switch the topic.

It always seems easier to avoid an argument, and we are just naturally worried about hurting the feelings of someone we love. We are also naturally anxious not to have our convictions all shaken up or our set ways challenged. But harbored resentments, even about insignificant things, can destroy love. They destroy love because when we only "talk" and don't communicate, when we are only partners instead of people who share our existence, we put the marriage relationship back up on the level of a surface thing.

The difference between talking partners and communicating lovers is that lovers will quarrel and "have it out" and eventually shape their values and ideas to each other. It's not great philosophical or theological issues which provoke crises, so much as it is little things. Little things are important for us to talk about. Will he come home when he said he would, instead of letting dinner get cold? What color will we paint the walls? Can we afford a new piece of furniture which she wants? Where will we go for a vacation? Should we rent or buy? Should we get a baby-sitter or save the money by staying home? These things seem so small, but they are things about which married people must think. They are the sort of things which begin to grind down married love to a dull war if they are not discussed and faced in open communication.

Storms

Storms are never pleasant, especially when they happen between people who want to love each other. That's the beautiful thing about marriage, though: Because of their love, two people can blow up at each other and still not have to worry that it's all over, that the relationship is off. In fact, many married people find out that the peace which follows an honest-to-goodness fight brings with it deeper love and greater understanding.

We all know we must care deeply for someone before we even bother to get angry with them, because hate and love are the same emotion. This is true even in marriage. The first two years of marriage for most people are a time for learning to survive storms, learning to live with the irritating side of a husband or wife, learning to like being with someone all the time, learning to share the existence of another human being who is just as irascible, just as unpredictable and stubborn, just as unstable, just as selfish, just as lovable as we are. The first two years are when we make mutual adjustments with great delicacy and great fights, great moments of intimacy and love, great periods of depression and elation. This is when we find out all about the person we love.

Secret Formulas

Our culture puts demands upon us as married people. The man, for instance, is supposed to be a competitor and he is supposed to live by the double standard of the business and financial world while remaining an uncorruptible, just man at home.

The woman is supposed to give up her active professional career in favor of children and home life. She is supposed to enjoy nursing babies, changing messy diapers and cleaning house.

Married people are supposed to do all sorts of things and act in specific ways. They are supposed to go to church together, they are supposed to vacation together, they are supposed to love each other wildly while also making money, raising children, visiting other people, setting up house, and taking an active part in community affairs. The demands are endless, and no one can come up with a magic formula for meeting these demands successfully.

No one can give a formula for happiness. But every couple find their formula, their secret formula. Secret because it's theirs and no one else's. Secret because they can't even always explain it. This is the real beginning of a happy, permanent marriage: the formula that a man and wife discover by themselves for sharing life and facing life together as long as they live.

How about this . . .

If you were a marriage counselor,
what would be the most important
thing you would want to tell a
newly married couple asking you
for general advice?

How long do you think engagements
should last, generally speaking?

How long do you think honeymoons
should last, generally speaking?

In your recollection of arguments
and breakdowns in communication
which have affected you, what
do you think were your biggest
mistakes?

11.

COMMUNICATION AND UNDERSTANDING

Communication is the key factor in any marriage; it takes about two days of married life to realize this. For that matter, it takes only a little reflection to realize that communication is the key to life and to any kind of personal relationships, because communication is the only way we can let another person know what's on our mind. Without communication we have no way of knowing what anyone else is thinking or feeling. Communication is our entrance into the world of others, and it is their doorway into ours.

Watching

There is a certain amount of sensitivity involved in the art of communicating. Some of the things to watch for, which might be the signal that someone is upset, would be the following:

— she is unusually quiet.
— she keeps dropping things.
— she is red in the face.
— she is jumpy.
— he keeps clenching his fist.
— he keeps avoiding you.
— he won't do anything except smoke and
  stare.

Listening

There are many more signs that things aren't
going right and that communication has broken
down. For example:
— he keeps switching the topic away from
  what you want.
— she keeps complaining about the same
  thing but you are sure she means something else. She may say how tired she is
  when she really means you haven't taken
  her to dinner in ages.
— he refuses to talk about money. The
  truth may be he doesn't have any.
— he wants to go golfing but you make him
  go to the store and help you shop. His
  silence may not signal contentment.
— she seems to act funny when she is all
  dressed up nice. That may be because she
  expects you to compliment her and
  notice how good she looks.
Watching, looking, and listening are not
easy skills to acquire, but they are the key to
what the other person is thinking. They are also
the key to avoiding unnecessary quarrels and mis-
understandings. Not all married people can read
each other's minds, only those who have
practiced a long time.

Breakdowns

No marriage can avoid the crises that come with occasional breakdowns in communication, any more than we can avoid having falling-outs with friends ever so often. The important thing is to realize when a breakdown has occurred and why it has occurred. Sometimes we feel someone is "crowding" us a little too much, and we break off with them until we feel comfortable again. Sometimes people are too big an influence upon us and we have to draw back a little to get our wits back. The same is true in love. Ever so often a husband or wife will get too domineering and we want to back off a little. The balance of love is delicate and sometimes needs readjusting.

There are other reasons for breakdowns in communication, of course, that are more common and are more serious. Sometimes breaking off communication is the final step in the hate process which began with disappointment or resentment. Sometimes we just honestly lose our temper and fly into a rage, ending all communication for some time. Whatever the reason, breakdown of communication is always more likely when there is more pressure upon the people involved. Money or job pressure is enough to break up a marriage because of the tension, fear and worry it generates. Sometimes the pressure of having too many children around the house without a break is enough to endanger a marriage, just as too long in the classroom can ruin a good teacher or cause a temporary crisis.

Repairs

Repairs are never pleasant, especially in

human relations. But our love life is going to be a whole series of repairs. The ingredients which go into making a good repair job are understanding, gentleness, sensitivity, and a sincere desire for the other person's happiness. That's what love is all about, anyway. What happens after the quarrel is more a proof of our love than we realize, because it is then we begin to find out just exactly how much the other person means to us and how much we mean to them.

Anyone can love us in our good moments, and we can love anyone else at their best. It's when things aren't very rosy that the real strength of our love is tested and proven for what it is. Friendships, whether romantic or otherwise, are proven by what we go through to maintain them. St. Peter found this out, and instead of letting his infidelity end his friendship with Christ, he did the repair job needed. There is a lesson here for all of us.

The Role

A husband is always wondering what his wife is thinking and why she does the things she does. He is always wondering, for example, how it feels to be pregnant. He usually wonders why she loves him, and sometimes he wonders if she loves him. What makes a woman tick? What makes a woman a woman? What is it like to be a woman at home, a mother, a career woman, a wife?

Feminine

A woman in our culture is different from women in other cultures. She isn't just a woman, she's an American woman. She's usually well educated, often college educated. She's usually highly skilled, and maybe she worked as a teacher, a nurse, or a social worker before she got married. She usually had more dreams than just becoming a wife and mother, although she certainly dreamed of being loved and having a family of her own.

As a wife, she is often an ex-career person, a woman who had planned to do great things in teaching or who enjoyed her job and who perhaps was able to keep it for some time after she married because she was so good. Most American women, if they are married, are beginning a second career, centered around a husband and children and a home. Most American women are frustrated.

A feeling of frustration, a feeling of being tied down and cooped up is not part of being a woman, nor is it the nature of woman to be tied down and cooped up. It is, however, the lot of most American women. The reason for this is that the American male is supposed to be the dominant figure on the scene.

An American woman is supposed to be beautiful, almost to specification. She is supposed to be curvy, sexy, personality-plus, delicate, young looking, sympathetic, gentle, loving, tender, full of energy, and a good cook. Just about all husbands find out that their wives are all of these things. But the woman who is only these things will often feel like she is only half a person. She will still want to *do* something, to be creative, to be more sociable than she is, to travel, to be needed and important in the community, to develop herself, to continue her education, to work with other people. She will often feel her husband has "the life" while she is stuck home with the screaming babies, helpless and frustrated, bewildered and tired.

Husbands, because our culture is what it is, feel the diapers and baby-sitting chores belong to her; household work is sissy stuff so men don't do it; the daily routine of a home is supposed to be easy and the man's work hard, so the husband forgets how badly his wife needs to "get out." And in the face of this, the wife begins to feel like a slave with no rights and no consideration, trapped into her situation.

The married woman in our culture thinks altogether differently from the unmarried girl in our culture. It's the difference between romantic dreams and romantic reality. Love looks so beautiful before it begins. Afterwards the real beauty of love, the reality of marriage, is much different from the dream.

Masculine

The man in our culture is supposed to be oversexed, just like the woman. He is also supposed to be rich, talented, dominant, personable, full of energy, cunning, clever, promising, and self-sufficient. He looks at a girl from a distance to find out how sexy she is; he looks for the figure and the physical beauty and he thinks of women in terms of pleasure. But as he enters into a serious relationship with a woman, he begins to look for love and understanding; he begins to notice the woman's inner beauty, and personality becomes the big consideration. He expects support and encouragement, understanding and steady comfort from his wife. He expects common interests and unwavering love.

The man is particularly sensitive to pressure

because he gets so much of it. He has a demanding boss, a demanding job, a very serious financial situation; he worries about the family he ends up with, he feels he is headed for a lifetime of work, worry, harassment, uncertainty, and fear. Everybody expects more of him than he is capable of furnishing. So the last thing he wants or ever expects is a wife who adds to his burdens by nagging, by arguing, by demanding. And that's usually the first thing he gets because she has so many troubles of her own.

The Difference

The difference between men and women is obviously more than physical and emotional. It's more a matter of cultural expectation and conditioning. We know all about the difference between our mothers and our fathers, and we know all about the difference between boys and girls, between men and women. But the way we see men and women before we are married and after we are married is the real surprise. Before marriage the stress in perceiving someone is on their lovable qualities and especially on their sexual and personal attractiveness. After marriage these are no longer the only or even the main ways of perceiving.

WHAT

Do

You

THINK ?

. . . . is the greatest joy for a man getting married? Why?

. . . . is the most difficult thing for a man getting married?

. . . . is the greatest joy for a woman getting married? Why?

. . . . is the most difficult thing for a woman getting married?

12.
BABIES

The easiest way to get free advice is to announce an engagement. The advice pours in. Friends, relatives, older married people, well-wishers, all feel an urge to pass on words of wisdom to the lovely young couple about to marry. People very often come up even at the wedding reception to talk about their formula for a successful marriage. People who have been married and ruined their marriage try to save the young couple from the same mistakes.

The wedding ceremony has much advice, too, coming out of the pages of the Old and New Testaments, reflecting the wisdom of ages. Eventually the advice boils down to sticking it out and never losing sight of the beauty we saw in our loved one in the first place. The advice also very frequently boils down to making and saving money.

Babies and the Budget

Babies are the first thing, naturally, that a young man and woman begin to think and talk about. Whether or not to have children hardly seems like a relevant question. Yet this can be a difficult decision because having babies is a difficult thing.

When someone deeply loves his husband or wife, it seems so logical for that love to bear fruit. Nothing is more beautiful than for a child to come forth from that love. The child is the living creation of married love. Because two people love each other so fully and so deeply, another beautiful, innocent little baby comes into being.

But once a baby is born, the wife can no longer work. If they were both working before the baby, this means the family income is reduced. Babies need cribs, playpens, clothing, and frequent physical checkups. The couple may also want to have a home of their own, to furnish it, and to settle down. This is when the doctor bills start to climb. This is when the food bills start to increase.

End of One Career, Beginning of Another

Most women have a job before marriage. Many go to college. Some plan a professional career. Often these jobs and plans carry over into marriage. The man, it is presumed, will have a lifelong career in a field of his choice, while the wife will carry on her career until the baby comes. When the baby comes, the end of the mother's career also arrives, and it often comes as a great shock.

Now instead of a woman, the wife has become a mother. Suddenly her whole existence is changed. Her focus has shifted from her husband and job and friends to her husband and her baby. No longer is she working with people and for people. Now she is working for her husband and her baby. Now her energy is spent day after day on her family. This is a radical change indeed, one which could not be prepared for, and one which has no equal. Becoming a mother has no way of being anticipated. The independence that comes with a job and with being young is gone in a flash, replaced by a darling little bundle of joy and by a new demand for immediate and constant love and care.

The Worries

Now the new mother is dependent. She is confined more than before to the house and to the neighborhood where she lives with her baby. She can go out of that house only if she takes the baby with her, or if somebody else will watch the baby. If she and her husband cannot afford baby-sitters, then she must look for a friend or a member of the family who will watch the baby. Otherwise she will not go out at all. She can never stop worrying about the baby's hunger and health. If she does, the baby is going to suffer. She assumes the responsibility for the life and well-being of a helpless, hungry, innocent little human being who will take life itself from her body and from her affection. Her entire day begins to focus around the needs of that baby.

The husband, too, finds life has changed. What man who loves his wife and child likes to see her tired and worn out all the time? He wants to help, and he needs to help. He finds himself changing diapers, heating bottles, baby-sitting. He finds himself wanting to make more money so things will be better. He finds himself starting to wonder if the original glow between him and his wife has been replaced by a baby. He finds himself starting to wonder about what it would be like to have a second and third baby, to be a "daddy" for the next 20 years, to be surrounded by screaming, crying, dirty, demanding babies. He begins to wonder if his beautiful wife is not becoming a worn out, tired out, washing woman, housecleaner, maid, and nurse.

It isn't very long after the babies start coming that parents start to wonder about morality. Birth control becomes a topic of discussion. Rhythm brings with it lots of tension, too, and even to speak of limiting the number of children born to the marriage makes the husband and wife think twice.

On the other hand, the marriage vows are a commitment to love and revere each other for a lifetime, and the commitment is one which hinges on a continuing love. Just how to treat each other and just how to love each other is a matter for some thought. Sexual morality, marriage morality, money morality, and personal integrity are not easy matters to think about. They are matched, of course, with great happiness and with the heights of love and affection. They are eased with the assurance that others have found their way clear. They are bearable because we live in perspective with God and with other people. The troubles and worries which babies bring get washed away in the sea of happiness that our children bring to us. Eventually we come to learn that people can never be truly a source of anything but goodness.

The First Baby

Daddy smokes half a pack of cigarettes the night the first baby is born. He walks right through a pair of shoes. He doesn't sleep for 48 hours, and he makes more phone calls than he ever made before in his life. He becomes a father, a worrier, a bragger, a provider, and cigar-smoker in a matter of minutes. He has been through all sorts of literature about birth, about conception, and about what happens to his wife. He may have gone to childbirth classes with her. He gets to know doctors he never thought he would meet. He's scared. And he's happy.

Mother goes through nine months of happy dreams and frightened visions of pain and suffering. Mother is pregnant, a new experience that nobody can really help her with. She has false labor and she worries that she may not know the real thing when it happens. But when the baby is born, a woman has become a mother, the anxiety passes away, and a child comes into the world.

The birth of the first baby is something every couple look forward to and are happy over. The utter thrill of feeling the first movements of the baby in the womb is surpassed by the love of holding the first baby in their arms and knowing it is theirs.

New People

To become a mother and father is to be created all over again. We emerge from this experience different people, new people, better people, changed people. The expectation of being loved gives way to the role of bestowing love. The creative urge is fulfilled and dreams come true. Girlhood and boyhood from this moment on are barely memories of the past.

No longer are we a young new couple starting out. No longer are we the young man or young woman who still has much to learn about marriage and life. No longer are we the newlyweds who need advice about how to love and what to do. Now we are men and women, husbands and wives, mothers and fathers. We're different, bigger, wiser. We have come of age and the baby we hold in our arms is young and appealing. Instead of being the center of the world, like we used to be, we begin to think of the baby as the center of the world. Our emotions and values, our outlooks and judgments undergo the kind of change that changes us. We start to fill out overnight as persons. We know what it means to be a man and what it means to be a woman. Sex is no longer the working criterion to measure ourselves or anyone else by; sex becomes submissive to life itself. Our baby, not ourselves, is life itself.

No Longer a Couple

Now we are no longer a couple. We have become a family. No longer are there just two people deeply in love. Now there are three, and one of us is a squawling, demanding, darling little creature who somehow manages to change all our plans and to affect the love relationship. The little baby changes the whole course of our lives. The baby changes us from a romantic young couple who got married into a family made up of parents who care for their child even before they care for each other. Now, instead of wondering where our love for each other will lead next, we begin to think about what kind of life our baby will have.

We begin to realize that our baby's personality will be what we make it to be right now. We begin to realize that our baby's intelligence depends on us; our baby's emotional growth depends on our own tenderness and maturity.

Our baby's life will be happy or less happy because of us. We begin to realize, without even trying, that to have our first baby is to do more than bring a human being into the world; it is to do more than just give someone existence. To have our first baby is to assume responsibility for our baby's continued existence. It is to assume responsibility for our baby's continuing and developing happiness.

To have a baby is to take responsibility for someone else's life and destiny. It is to accept a new relationship that will never end. It is to permanently bring another person into the love affair that began with our first date and will continue even after death. To have our first baby is to become more like God than we've ever been before.

A person who is hungry for love or emotionally disturbed may find it almost to be at peace with a new baby. A person who needs more than he or she gives may never be able to be a father or mother, because he may never be able to respond to a dependent creature such as their first baby will surely be. Because the husband and wife are the security base for their baby, their immaturity can keep the baby from developing into a full human person. This begins to dawn with the birth of a first baby. We begin to realize we should not be parents until we feel sure enough of ourselves to respond fully to the groping, frowning little human being called a baby. When we hold our first child in our arms and hands, we know we are not ready. We know it is an impossible challenge. We know it will take more love than we have. Yet, we wouldn't want it any other way.

Do you know . . .

how much it costs to have a baby in
the first year of marriage in
your community?

how much a family with four
children needs to earn in
your community in order
to stay above the poverty
line?

what kind of career you want
in life?

what is the one thing you want
more than anything else in
your lifetime? Why?

13.

MONEY: THE PERENNIAL PROBLEM

The very first piece of advice newlyweds hear is to save their money. One of the first things people tell them is to watch out for money fights. Yet, in the glow of the honeymoon, most couples think such problems will never come to them. Even if poverty is staring them in the face, they cannot believe money tensions could ever overcome the strength and healing warmth of their married love or drive them to fierce, long-lasting, bitter quarrels. But this is precisely what happens more times than not.

Things always seem to go so well at first. Sometimes a little unexpected cash shows up in the wedding presents. Sometimes the parents "come through" with a surprise endowment or a goodwill loan. Often the new bride is able to work, providing a double income. Occasionally there is money saved from before the wedding, and always there is the prospect of promotions, raises, or better jobs just around the corner. Whatever the variations, things usually look good enough after the wedding to make rent payments, down payments, house payments, credit union payments, and charge account payments less foreboding and smaller than they really are. Besides that, even if worse came to worse and a sacrifice were demanded — such as moving into a smaller, older, less comfortable house or apartment or trailer — that would be such a small price to pay for the joy of living as husband and wife, for the joy of being together, for the joy of finally being married.

Doubts

Slowly, however, doubts begin to creep in. The woman begins to suspect she is pregnant or that she wants to get pregnant. She doubts that she could continue teaching or doing whatever she does if she were pregnant. She begins to doubt, too, that there is enough money for the new baby and she begins to worry about what a new baby needs. She also begins wondering how to get her husband used to the idea of only one income in the near future.

The husband begins to doubt, too. Maybe he is wondering if he will ever finish school. Maybe the promotion doesn't come, or maybe he starts to think about the bills a first and second and third baby will add to the already heavy stack of bills coming in each month. He was just getting things paid off. Maybe they need a new car or more furniture. Maybe a vacation will have to be drastically changed in order to save money. He starts to wonder if maybe a little money could be saved on entertainment or groceries or on clothes.

Gradually doubts become worries, and worries become fear. Where money is concerned, even the worst fear seems to come true, ard the best-planned alternatives to disaster inevitably evaporate. It gets harder and harder to save money, and bills seem to come faster and faster. Subtly the goal of saving great amounts of money becomes so altered that the big thing each month is to pay all the expenses and still not fall any farther behind.

Hidden Agendas

Of course, the process of learning to worry about money is not nearly as pleasant as it sounds and it is *never* peaceful. Worries about money mean differences about how much to tip on the rare nights out; they mean squabbles about whether or not to get a new car or to wait; they mean arguments about whether or not he should play poker or go golfing, or whether or not she should go shopping so often. Money worries mean serious arguments about how much insurance to get, about how much to spend on Christmas presents, how much to spend on shoes, how often to go to the doctor.

Even more seriously, however, money worries mean a steady, grinding source of tensions that erupt over unrelated things. Money tension means fighting about whether or not to have intercourse, whether or not to use birth control, whether or not to have company. It means squabbling about everything under the sun except what is the real worry or the real source of anger and frustration. It means a hidden agenda underlying nearly every quarrel and every irritation. It means a lot of adjustment that often never takes place because hidden agendas are difficult to deal with.

Hidden agendas which revolve around financial insecurity account for many of today's divorces — divorces which occur in spite of the fact that the husband and wife still love each other but somehow are no longer compatible. They are no longer compatible in fact not with each other, but with the third partner whose name is worry and whose calling card is tension and whose presence is undetected.

Times — They Are Changing

When it comes to tension and a complicated life, times have changed for the worse—as the high sale of Excedrin and various other pills and drugs demonstrates. This tension falls on the man at work and the woman at home. For the newly married couple, this means the wife has a very difficult time, indeed. Her role as housewife is frustrating and tends to bottle her up in her home and inside herself. She must manage a double role if she works; whether she works or not, she inherits a role that ties her to the kitchen, the children, the laundry, and her home in a time when women are being oriented in school and in general to be professional, to be creative, to be socially free, and to get out of the home.

The woman's love for her husband today leads her into direct conflict with her original aspirations to "be somebody," to be creative and free, and to live a good, rewarding life. On top of that, her husband comes home with his own tensions and problems, harried and fatigued. She doesn't see him all day long; when he finally gets home they quarrel; when they get to bed she feels mixed emotions; before she knows it the next day has arrived and it's time to start the treadmill all over.

The more children she has, the more she is apt to feel trapped, and the more her husband is tempted to think about how beautiful she used to be and how much money his family is costing, about how much money he doesn't have. Somehow the thought always comes back to money.

Before long, it is time to move, and before long it is time to move again. (One fifth of American families move every year.) Mobility adds to financial instability and brings new social adjustments, new relationships to strike up, new everything. Children change the couple to a mother and father, bringing yet new roles and new dimensions of concern. And so on and so on. It all adds up, in the end, to a great burden on the woman, a great burden made extremely heavy by the perennial problem for both of them, money.

When it's all over, we finally begin to realize why love is so important. In fact, we start to realize that untried and unproved love is no love at all. The worries, the cares, the perennial headaches — that's why we have marriage, to pull us through this life in one piece. When the marriage is filled with love, we come through looking like champs.

Do you agree . . . .

. . . . that the average American married woman is very deeply frustrated and worried?

. . . . that the average young married American man is deeply frustrated and worried?

. . . . with the main contention of this chapter, that money problems lie at the root of many other marriage problems?

. . . .

If you had a choice, would you rather be living now, a hundred years ago, or a hundred years in the future? Why?

14.
THE WORKING
MOTHER...

When your grandmother was a young girl, she knew what her life would be like. She would marry, raise a family, and take care of her husband. Her family would be her contribution to society. She probably looked with scorn on the "working mother" idea. She felt a woman's place was in the home, taking care of her family. She probably did not feel much need to read and to "keep up." She probably felt little obligation to contribute socially, other than by doing a good job with her children and working hard.

Psychology

A number of factors have changed the role of woman in our society from what it was in years gone by. One such factor is the growth of psychology. Psychology is a very young science, when we consider it in terms of the evolution of mankind. It has only been during the last few decades that ordinary people began to have some knowledge of the basic needs which must be met if they are to grow as persons. It is only very recently that psychology has made it possible to understand role expectations and their effect upon the individual.

Psychology has made it plain, only recently, that women as well as men need to grow as individuals. Even more important, psychology has made obvious to all the implications of this fact. It is these implications which are changing the acceptable roles of women from what used to be to what is.

Business for a long time has recognized the fact that a man works best when he is performing a job he likes. Many companies use a sophisticated battery of tests to help men in positions where they will be most effective and happy. It is only recently, however, that the same principles have been recognized in regard to the woman at home. Women, just as men, have different temperaments and inclinations which require different occupations and roles for the individual to be happy and effective. Every woman cannot be a successful domestic wife and mother.

Betty Friedan published *The Feminine Mystique* a few years ago, making this very point. The book caused a great debate all across the nation. One side of the debate saw Mrs. Friedan and other advocates of the modern woman confronting those on the other side who feel all women should find their place in the home and stay there. Betty Friedan argued for the creative, renewing aspects of a job outside the home. In the great middle were most women, who, while remaining housewives, worked part time or had other creative and intellectual outlets to satisfy their need for personal growth and dignity. Such women were immensely relieved that Mrs. Friedan and others were pointing out the fact that there was nothing wrong with them if they failed to become enthralled with hours of cleaning. Finally it was being publicly acknowledged that housewives could get frustrated and discouraged at the endless, trying activities involved in caring for small children, in constant housework, and in the drudgery of home tasks. The debate was never settled, but the point was made. Psychology had made its impact.

Education

A second factor which is causing a change in

the role of woman is the growing educational level of women. Many more women than before are now going on to college or to some type of career training schools. Career training schools are teaching women professional skills which allow them to function in a professional way and to be treated as important professional persons.

At colleges and universities across the country, women are acquiring not only professional skills but also a broad knowledge base. This knowledge base is enabling them to understand themselves and their society better, which in turn is enabling them to love and respond to love in deeper and more varied ways than before. Today's woman sees herself as an intelligent, educated individual, and she tastes the excitement of pursuing new knowledge. She leaves college desiring to keep up with current changes in the world and to take a hand in creating those changes and that world.

From her understanding of society and of what is happening in her society, today's woman is experiencing a new sense of commitment. She is accepting an obligation to do something about community housing needs. She may feel a commitment to see that the community has access to more cultural forms. Whatever shape it takes, her sense of involvement and commitment is a fact. Today's woman no longer considers herself part of an isolated family unit. She feels an obligation to the larger society because she belongs to the larger society.

Jobs

New employment patterns have also caused a change of role for women. Increasing opportunity has opened to women jobs which were always closed to them before. There is still inequity in both salaries (as compared to men) and jobs available, but more and more jobs are being opened up to women, and salaries are slowly increasing. Because it is becoming more and more possible for a woman to find a job she likes, many women are beginning to work in a professional capacity before marriage and when they are first married. They are treated as professionals. They dress like professionals and they think of themselves as professionals.

With marriage, and especially with the birth of children, a young woman can't help but feel acutely the drastic change in life style. Small children take continuous care. They need affection, discipline, and guidance on an around-the-clock basis. They demand constant emotional and physical attention. Their daytime nap period may be the only time during the entire day when she can manage to get any housework done. After they have gone to bed and she has tied up loose ends for that day, she is usually too exhausted to read or do anything personally creative. No matter how much she loves her children, there will be times when their constant demands really put pressure on her.

Her activity rate has soared, but her creativity and professional life, her feeling of "accomplishing something worthwhile" have evaporated. She now will spend hours each day cleaning all the dirt her family drags into her home. Cleaning is a tremendous contrast to her former professional role, a contrast made all the more demanding by the spotless, perfectly furnished homes constantly being beamed forth in all the media. This subtle conscious and subconscious pressure dictates that the good life include a spotless house, beautifully groomed children and a meticulous, weed-free yard.

The educated woman has built into her from school the pressure to keep up with the current events, something which takes time. It also takes time to read and to become and remain an intelligent conversationalist. Today's woman is likely, then, to feel pressures her grandmother did not feel. She is likely to feel conflict, since she can't do all the things expected of her all the time.

Even a deeper understanding of child psychology takes more out of today's women. It takes a great deal more patience and a great deal more time to deal with children in a manner which encourages their personal development. Many parents have deep guilt feelings about failure with their children, whereas Grandmother simply made them behave.

No one is a perfectly balanced individual. No one is a perfect parent. Parents can try too hard. Mistakes used to be water over the dam, and Grandmother never worried about them, but for today's parents and especially for today's mothers, mistakes are serious failings.

Some Mothers Should Work

A mother who is so frustrated that she is on the point of a breakdown, or who resigns herself to being bitter or unhappy, would be better off finding a baby-sitter and going back to work. Quality of love is much more important than quantity. Bitterness and continual irritation with children can only result in making the children insecure and frustrated, whereas less time spent with her children but spent more lovingly can in the long run be better for the children and the mother.

Going back to work will present some new problems, of course. It will demand more organization of time, for one thing. It may also mean getting help with the housework or hiring a maid. Sometimes, successful women may threaten their husbands who are less successful, causing deep bitterness in the marriage relationship.

For some mothers, the problems to be surmounted in having a job cause just as many difficulties as the pressures of staying at home as a housewife. There are other alternatives to staying home besides going back to work as a professional. Some of these alternatives involve creative outlets such as the arts, classes, developing a taste for literature or working part time. The options, in any case, are not as many as they ought to be but they are increasing all the time. This is good, because it means a woman's chances of developing as a full person are increasing all the time.

OK, but . . .

What kinds of creative outlets are considered acceptable in your community for young married mothers?

What kind of frustration did your mother experience in adapting to the role of wife and mother?

Do you think the problems of being a mother have been overstated in the chapter? Why?

Are women in practice equal to men in our culture?

COMPROMISE

15.

John Kennedy in many ways stood for the things many people wish they could stand for. He campaigned hard for things many people used to work for before they got married. He was always trying to figure out how to raise the incomes of low-income people; he was forever talking about ways to make it possible for people trapped by illness, poverty, poor jobs, or handicaps to upgrade themselves. He believed that the black man had been denied his birthright as an American, and he did more than just talk about injustice.

Married people, on the whole, find themselves more concerned about their families than about the poor or the sick and suffering of this world or even of their own town. Many young married people find themselves living in suburbia for the sake of their children or because of their job. They find themselves turning their backs on those less fortunate than themselves.

There is a certain amount of guilt experienced when this happens. These same young people, only a few years before, may have been totally immersed in work with people, work with children, work in the community. They may have been in the Peace Corps or in any number of creative projects designed to wipe away some of the human suffering in this world.

Look at the great peace movements sweeping through colleges today; look at the courageous students taking part in all sorts of demonstrations and pressure tactics designed to stop human misery. Yet, these very same students a few years later will be married, will be parents, and will drop out of the various movements in which they believe.

Ideals

Marriage plans usually include generous doses of discussion about what is important in life. Planned into the marriage are deep ideals, such as a desire to be generous and open with our many friends, and perhaps even spending a number of years in the service of other people. It seems so logical, when falling in love, to feel closer than ever to those who need us and those who will never be as happy as we.

Deep as the ideals may be, there still comes a day just a few years later when we wake up and suddenly realize that we haven't done a thing to *really* help anyone besides ourselves and our children in the last few years. We begin to realize we are part of the vast silent majority or the selfish minority or the noncommitted and non-concerned. We realize our job or money or our love life or something has become such an over-riding concern that our focus has changed and the ideals we carried with us into marriage have somewhere and somehow died or at least died down. Much to our horror, there will come a day when we will realize we have become part of the establishment or the middle class or what-ever.

Then start the gnawing, nagging doubts and guilt. How can we afford concern with the poor when our debts qualify us as poor? How can we demonstrate for open housing when we live in a closed neighborhood or when everyone we know lives in a comfortable home and none of our friends is poor or of a different race? How can we be concerned with sick people when the only sicknesses we know are the ailments of our children or those of somebody at work who has cancer or a heart condition? How can we work for peace when our income tax supports war and when, possibly, we think war has become necessary?

The questions won't go away. Eventually they boil down to the question which absolutely won't go away: "Am I really Christian? Are we really Christians?" Put the question another way, and it comes out to be "What would St. Paul do if he were in my shoes?" or "If I had my life to start all over again, what would I do differently?"

Trapped?

The truth of the matter is that our culture and economic structure are not particularly geared to encourage Christian idealism or any kind of idealism. Our high schools and colleges foster idealism and vision, but the economy and the culture kill it off in married people and in families. Survival becomes the first law of marriage; survival becomes the only law, once there are children and a job worth not losing. Survival hardens our judgment and narrows our generosity.

Worry and survival dull our sensitivity and trap us into doing things we didn't believe in or endorse before. The movements which characterize our social patterns, housing patterns, and economic patterns catch us, too. We find ourselves thinking upward and outward. The unspoken law becomes "every man for himself" and "God helps those who help themselves" and "don't rock the boat — it might land on you" and "don't get involved" and "let's wait and see" and "I haven't got time" and "it will all work out."

We are slowly but surely made to believe that there isn't much we can do about anything except learn to live with it and hope we and our family make it through safe and sound.

Betrayal or Realism?

There are those who roundly condemn the process just described. Many consider this process of changing one's values from idealistic goals to survival as a dry rot creeping over America and killing the souls of us all.

There are others who see this process as adjustment to reality, as inevitable, as the natural consequence of a free enterprise economy which is designed to force people to be responsible for their own well-being in a competitive society. Many people claim that devotion to one's wife or husband and children is enough for anyone, and that obligations to others take second place if any at all.

The judgment must be made by each of us, but one thing is certain: The vision and ideals of our early life somehow get lost during early marriage as new pressures and concerns emerge. Whether or not they will be permanently lost or repressed or buried depends on each one of us. It is not being human to shrug it all off and say this kind of decision is out of our hands. Our destiny always lies with us, and the world will always be the kind of world *we* make it to be.

No matter what happens, it will always be true that we have only one life to live. When our life is over, we will look back and wonder where it went. Indeed, long before our life is over, we will begin looking back, but it will already be too late to do it all over again. The cruelest judgment of all will come from within us, and it will be the judgment which our own idealism will pass upon the things we did in spite of ourselves. St. Paul once said he thought he did the things he did not want to do, and the things he most wanted to do he left undone. That's the kind of thoughts we will face, married or not, but most of all if we are married.

The conflict between realism and idealism will never go away. But only we will be able to answer for ourselves as to whether we betrayed our ideals or were simply being realistic. Maybe there is a difference. But maybe the difference is to be found in the kind of reality we created. Is our reality made up of all the human beings with whom we share a destiny, or is it made up of only those with whom we wish to share a destiny?

Frankly now . . .

Can you think of any ideal you have given up during the past year? If so, why did you give it up?

Do you think your parents have had to compromise their ideals for your sake?

Does the end ever justify the means?

What do you think are the most glaring examples of a clash in idealism between the young people of today and the old people of today?

16.
JOURNEY'S END

Marriage has all sorts of definitions, and the things said about marriage probably take up more books than any other topic in the world. There is nothing new to be said about marriage. All that has been said is all that needs to be said, but what remains is for people to realize over and over again what their marriage is really all about. One such thing we all need to realize over and over again is that our marriage is a whole bundle of revelations.

Revelation

In marriage, for example, we are continually revealing ourself to the one we love. We do this physically, of course, and we also do it emotionally and intellectually. Self-revelation is a sign of deep trust, for the more someone knows about us the more vulnerable we become, and the more he knows how to hurt us. In love we reveal ourselves to such an extent that we depend upon each other for our security. As we grow, so does the revelation grow.

We are a sign to our children, too, for even when we are not trying to communicate, our children are "drinking us in." Everything we believe in they will believe in; everything we think about they will think about; everything we stand for will mean something to them. Our values will, in the main, be the things they consider important.

Our children will think of God in terms of us and they will see authority through the authority which we exercise toward them. They will see other people with the kind of love we gave to them, and they will be able to love and relate to others in direct proportion to the way in which we loved them and cared for them. Their emotional life will be built upon the affection we lavish upon them, and they will see the world the way they saw us.

Our Legacy

Our marriage is revelation not only for ourselves and for our children but also for our friends. As our friends look at us, they will begin to see what love means, and from watching us they will learn how to love each other, just as we watch other people and learn. We become a revelation, by our love for each other and people around us, of our worth and their worth. The word "love" gets translated by our relationship from an abstract dreamy ideal into real understandable friendship and affection. Actions begin

136

to speak more eloquently than words, and the people around us start to know they are important.

Because of our love for our friends and because of the love we have for each other and for our children, the people around us begin to believe that God loves them, too, because they begin to see what love is. We become one of the vehicles of revelation about God. We furnish the experience and the frame of reference for love to be understandable. Because of us, other people can take themselves more seriously and they can begin to believe how much they really mean to others. This is the way communities are built and this is the way we all need to develop in personal dimensions.

One of the greatest of the Jewish philosophers, Martin Buber, spent his whole lifetime thinking about how people relate to one another, and about the part love plays in our lives. He decided that our existence is colored by those around us so much that without other people we would dry up inside. What happens when people enter into relationships with each other is mutual growth. Without the relationship, neither we nor the people around us are happy, and no one exists in their true fullness. We draw our strength from one another. For this reason, we live more and more fully by entering into more and more relationships with people.

When a friendship is broken off, part of us dies and part of the friend dies. When a new friendship is formed, we add that much to our being and the new friend grows a little more, too. Human existence is a network of friendships and meaningful relationships, and to the extent that it is, it is meaningful. When human existence becomes characterized by a lack of friendship, to that extent it is meaningless and people begin to wonder if life is worth anything at all.

Marriage, in this context, becomes a foundation stone for the happiness of many human beings, and the help by which we can live as full, happy people. Upon the marriage relationship hinge the beauty and goodness of human existence. Upon our married life is built the happiness of ourselves, our children, our friends, and our associates. From our marriage love begins to radiate to other people, and from our marriage comes the ever-renewed revelation that people really do count more than anything else.

A Journey Together

In the last scene of the movie *The Long Grey Line,* the leading character has become an old man. His wife has just died and been buried. The old man, having lived his whole lifetime with her, cannot get used to the loneliness. He wanders out to the parade ground of West Point, where they used to walk together often, and where, on many Sunday afternoons, they would watch the dress parade. As he gazes out across the open spaces, his mind starts to wander back over the years and he starts to hear the music once again. He sees his young wife, skirt in hand, dancing to the music and laughing, flirting with him and the others, arm in arm, reeling off first this dance then that. Other scenes of his life come back to him, too, and his wife is there in front of him once again, not old, not gone, but young and happy, laughing and gay, beautiful and with him forever.

The scene from the movie is a common scene, indeed, for people who have been married a long time. By the time the end of life comes, we too will begin to realize just how much we share the existence of those we love, and we will begin to realize that marriage is truly shared existence.

Many older married people even begin to resemble each other. Often they are able to read each other's mind, and they instinctively sense when the other is happy or sad, when something is wrong, or when the other is upset. It is as though one mind were beginning to emerge where before there were two. It is as though one love were beginning to spring up where before there were two lovers; one personality beginning to flow forth where before there were two. When death comes, so much was the common existence shared that many older married people have nothing left to live for. They want to be reunited with the person they loved all their life, and death becomes not something to fear but something to wait for eagerly because it will bring them back to their loved one.

Marriage brings us together with the person we love forever. Wherever they go, we will go, and whatever they do, we will share, for we will never again part. Our destinies are merged when we marry, and all that remains is for us to work out that destiny. So true is this that we can reasonably expect to spend eternity together. It would be absurd to think that one of the married couple could go to heaven while the other could end up in hell, for this would mean that they really did not share their existence here on earth. It is almost impossible to share a common existence and still not share a common destiny. It is very difficult, indeed, to live with someone and not share his values. At the same time, though, we not only share but we shape each other's values, so that it doesn't take long before both married people are operating upon the same basic values and outlooks.

We Live On

Not only do we share a common existence and a common destiny as married people, but we live on together. Certainly in eternity we live on together, in a love deeper and more beautiful than our love here on earth. But we also live on in this life after our death, and this is in our children. Our children will carry our name and our memory with them through their lives, and our children's children will do the same, so that from generation to generation for a long, long time our name lives on.

Not only will our name live on, but we will survive in the memory of our good works. The things we do in our lifetime will live on after us, and in them we, too, shall live on. It is like the great cathedrals of Europe which have lasted centuries after their builders. The builders will live as long as the cathedrals last. As long as the good things we have achieved in life continue to bear fruit and to make this world a better place, we shall live on in them.

It probably takes a whole lifetime of marriage to realize how much of a blessing the Jewish wedding blessing really is. Part of this blessing used to be read over the bride and groom at Catholic weddings, and what was wished upon the married couple was hard to realize then. When we look back and start counting our blessings, though, we will begin to realize how happy indeed was the journey together. What was wished upon us as we began the journey comes true throughout most of the journey, and at the end we will remember the beginning. When the end comes we will realize where we are traveling. The blessing, you may recall, goes in part like this:

> "May the God of Abraham, the God of Isaac, the God of Jacob bless you and keep you. May he grant you health. May he send you true friends to stand by you. May you see your children's children to the third and fourth generation. And when this life is over, may he grant you everlasting happiness."

For the wife, the blessing continues:

> "May she be the beloved of her children. May she be grave in her modesty as was Sarah, may she be fruitful as was Rebecca. May she be the beloved of her husband as was Rachel. May cares never cause her to worry. May she reap the rewards of a happy life."

Such is the journey we call marriage. . .

Can you remember your grandparents?
Do your parents ever talk about
                    them?
Do you know any married people
whose love radiates out to their
children, friends and
                    associates?

What do you think is the most
outstanding quality in the

marriage of the married couple whom you most admire?

If you were a priest and were supposed to make up your own wedding blessing instead of using a prescribed form, what would be the blessing you would make up and pray over people whose wedding you were blessing?